UNLOCKING THE PROPERTY MARKET

UNLOCKING THE PROPERTY MARKET

The 7 KEYS TO PROPERTY INVESTMENT SUCCESS

JOHN LINDEMAN

Wrightbooks
A Wiley Brand

First published in 2015 by Wrightbooks

An imprint of John Wiley & Sons Australia, Ltd

42 McDougall St, Milton Qld 4064

Office also in Melbourne

Typeset in 11/15pt ITC Giovanni Std by Aptara, India

© John Lindeman 2015

The moral rights of the author have been asserted

National Library of Australia Cataloguing-in-Publication data:

Creator:	Lindeman, John, author.
Title:	Unlocking the Property Market: the 7 keys to property investment success / John Lindeman.
ISBN:	9780730319818 (pbk.)
	9780730319825 (ebook)
Notes:	Includes index.
Subjects:	Real estate investment — Australia.
	Real estate business — Australia.
Dewey Number:	332.63240994

Cover and internal image (key) by Tarchyshnik/iStockphoto.com

Cover design by Wiley

Printed in Australia by Ligare Book Printer

10 9 8 7 6 5 4 3 2 1

Disclaimer
The material in this publication is of the nature of general comment only, and does not represent professional advice. It is not intended to provide specific guidance for particular circumstances and it should not be relied on as the basis for any decision to take action or not take action on any matter which it covers. Readers should obtain professional advice where appropriate, before making any such decision. To the maximum extent permitted by law, the author and publisher disclaim all responsibility and liability to any person, arising directly or indirectly from any person taking or not taking action based on the information in this publication.

To Carolyn

Contents

Foreword   *ix*

About the author   *xiii*

Introduction   *xv*

Key 1: Understand how the housing market works   1

Key 2: Find areas with the best growth potential   33

Key 3: Discover where and when to buy   63

Key 4: Narrow down your search   95

Key 5: Decide what to buy   125

Key 6: Determine how much to pay   139

Key 7: Know the best time to sell   155

Further resources   *173*

Glossary   *179*

Index   *183*

Foreword

I've probably heard every single property 'strategy' around. From sermons on property prices doubling every seven to ten years (they generally don't) to bluff and bluster on buying off-the-plan units and banking on prices rising rapidly during construction (they generally don't) so you can on-sell before settlement and make a motza. Yeah, right.

In 10 years of property journalism, I've experienced two property booms, one bust, one flood and one cyclone and here we are in 2015 in the midst of the cycle all over again with many of these dubious 'strategies' snaring unwary investors yet again.

With so much 'noise' and so many self-proclaimed 'experts' in a rising market, that's why it continues to be imperative that investors access the best and most objective property data, analysis and commentary.

And this is where John Lindeman comes in. John is one of a very select group of columnists in the *Australian Property Investor*

(*API*) magazine, which has been the number-one publication for property investment for some 18 years. *API* has a large and loyal following who turn to us every month for trusted and impartial property investment advice and we only have the best of the best in our magazine.

John's exclusive research column is by far and away one of the most read, and re-read, sections of the magazine each and every month. Many of our readers have been property investors for decades and they recognise a kindred soul in John's research and his ability to analyse complex data sets but explain them relatively simply.

As editor of *API*, it's my good fortune to read John's column before anyone else does, and I must admit that even after many years in the property game myself, without fail, each month I learn something new. From how to identify slingshot suburbs and which season is best to buy and sell, to the truth behind historical price-growth patterns (which is that regularly spouted, but incorrect furphy about prices doubling much quicker than they really do), John's property insight continues to teach me how to be a better and more successful investor month after month.

Personally, what I admire most about John is the depth of his research and analysis as well as the fact that he's an active and successful property investor himself. And he's been around long enough to have an investment philosophy that anyone can understand. John's methodology includes analysing types of property, price ranges, location, as well as fluctuations in sales and listings to easily identify market changes and trends. He then passes all of that lovely research over to us, so we can benefit and profit from it — like in this book, for example.

Unlocking the Property Market is a continuation of John's research columns and offers valuable information for investors on how the housing market works, where to find areas with the best growth potential, where and when to buy, how to narrow down your search, what to buy, how much to pay and when to sell.

I have no doubt that by understanding these steps to investment success, investors will not only be more informed about the market but they'll also become more skillful when searching for their next property to ensure they make the best and most profitable buying decision.

In person and on the page, John is astute, knowledgeable and one of the good guys of the property investment sector. I trust you will learn as much from him as I have.

Nicola McDougall
Editor
Australian Property Investor magazine

About the author

John Lindeman is seen as the market researcher that other property experts go to for detailed insights into the Australian housing market.

It was John's early property investment mistakes that made him determined to find out how the housing market works and how property investors can get the most benefit. His quest of discovery included ten years of professionally researching the housing market with major data providers and personally analysing the dynamics of every type of housing market in Australia.

With the research done, John revealed the secrets of his discoveries in his best-selling book, *Mastering the Australian Housing Market*, which became a landmark publication for investors. His column on housing market research has featured in *Australian Property Investor* magazine every month since 2011 and he is a regular contributor to Ken Turner's *Real Estate Talk*, Michael Yardney's *Property Update* and Alan Kohler's *Eureka Report*.

It is John's special understanding of how the housing market works that sets him apart from other analysts and commentators. John explains that success comes from knowing where to buy and when to sell — that timing the market offers investors a much faster path to achieving their goals than buying, holding and hoping for growth to occur.

John's mission is to share with other investors his unique insights into the nature and direction of the Australian residential property market so that they can avoid the mistakes investors commonly make and obtain the best possible results.

Introduction

Although housing investment provides reliable returns for thousands of property investors, Australian Taxation Office figures reveal that most investors lose money on housing, even when the housing market grows in value. I have spoken with many of these disillusioned people at property seminars, expos and workshops in recent years, and listened to their experiences. It is clear that the difference between the successful and unsuccessful investors doesn't stem from the capacity of the property market to generate excellent returns, but from the choices that investors make. Every housing investor can make decisions to ensure that they receive the best possible results — so why do so many take paths that lead to losses and, in the worst cases, financial ruin?

The answer lies in the information that investors rely on. Some investors make decisions based on their personal view of the market, without doing any real property market research at all. They might buy an investment property near their home so that they can keep an eye on it, or buy a house where they holiday each year because it's such an attractive location. Others buy in a remote town because they have heard that a new mine is opening and prices are about to shoot skywards. Maybe their friend bought a property somewhere and tells them that prices have doubled in recent years, or a brochure they receive informs them that properties in a certain new development are selling like hot cakes and if they're not quick, they'll miss out. These are all very good reasons to conduct further research, but they should never form the basis of a decision to purchase. If you are a property investor, you need to have a clear understanding of what results you want to achieve and how the housing market can help you to secure them.

Property investment is unlike purchasing a home. People don't generally buy and sell dwellings to make money from capital growth or cash flow, but to make a home. They may not buy in areas that are going up in price or where rent demand is rising, but where they can afford or prefer to live in. They don't sell to realise a profit, but because it's time to move to a bigger home, in a better location, or to a retiree destination. This gives you, the investor, a huge advantage because you are competing with buyers and sellers whose motives are not profit-based. But to take advantage of this, you need to use an investment strategy that is appropriate to your personal situation.

Housing investment can provide income from rent *or* capital growth from price rises — and these are fundamentally different approaches. Many investors fail to grasp this essential truth and, as a result, their investments fail to generate a profit. If there's one rule that you should never lose sight of, it is to always borrow for passive growth and never for cash flow. This is the essential difference between good and bad debt and, properly applied, it will turn property investment into a profitable lifelong journey.

Let's assume that you, or maybe your children, are new investors who have scraped up just enough money for a deposit. Your strategy should be to buy a property that is going to rise in price as quickly as possible, turning the growth in its value into profit. This is called *leveraging*, because while you contribute only the deposit when you buy, you only repay the loan amount when you sell and keep the difference, less costs and taxes.

To work for you, this strategy needs only two fundamentals. First, you must be able to make regular interest repayments on the borrowed money, and second, the property must substantially grow in price during the time that you own it. This means you should buy in a suburb where high price-growth is about to occur. Timing is everything; not just buying at the right time, but also selling just before the growth comes to an end. Some investors try to use this strategy by buying in risky areas such as mining towns and ports, but that's just speculation and not at all necessary. The idea is to buy in suburbs where the demand from prospective buyers is growing faster than the number of properties available, because that's where prices are likely to rise quickly.

Although you may start this strategy with just enough deposit for one property, your equity grows each time you ride the wave of price-growth, enabling you to buy more properties and repeat the process. Each time this happens, you are using the borrowed money to make more money, which is why this is called good debt. This strategy puts you far ahead of an investor who holds the same property over a long period of time, hoping for growth to occur.

At some stage, when you have amassed considerable capital by buying, selling and then buying properties again in high price-growth areas, you will want to change to a cash-flow strategy. This is when you gradually swap your portfolio of investment properties from those with growth potential to those that will assure you of a reliable income stream. In other words, you now use your equity to buy high rent-yield properties, which you own without any debt, in strong rental demand areas. There's little point to borrowing if your aim is cash flow, because the interest on the borrowed money robs you of cash flow and can even result in a negative return—this is bad debt. These two different investment strategies can only be generated by certain types of housing in specific localities. This means that where you buy, what you buy and when you sell play a crucial part towards helping you achieve your desired results.

Unfortunately many investors rely on the ineffective and even inaccurate selection and prediction methods the property investment industry is rife with. Some commentators will tell you that the market will always perform as it has in the past and that price increases eventually and evenly flow almost anywhere, so it doesn't matter where or when you buy. Others may talk about the housing market cycle or property clock to show you that growth and decline come and go like the seasons. Some experts will claim that a lack of recent price-growth proves that growth is way overdue and the market is about to boom, while others will tell you the opposite; that recent price rises identify hot suburbs that are about to go gangbusters. There are even some who claim that the property market behaves in mysterious ways only known to a select few. If you ask them to explain, they'll tell you it's far too difficult for you to understand, but they'll give you a glimpse for a price, of course.

Housing is the biggest investment most of us ever make. You have a right to know what to believe about these seemingly contradictory and confusing theories, but also why *timing* the market, rather than *time in* the market, is the most profitable strategy you can adopt.

The tools revealed in this book distil nearly two decades of my personal and professional research into the nature and likely direction of the housing market. They are the essence of the more than 50 monthly articles I have written for *Australian Property Investor* magazine as their research columnist since 2011. They will empower you to test what you read or hear and take the best possible course of action. These seven keys will unlock the door to the property market for you, explaining:

➤ how the housing market works

➤ where to find areas with the best growth potential

➤ where and when to buy

➤ how to narrow down your search

➤ what to buy

➤ how much to pay

➤ when to sell.

I trust that this book will help you make the best possible housing investment decisions.

Understand how the housing market works

This key unlocks the door to the secrets of the housing market, showing how to get the greatest benefits when you invest in residential property. You will:

➤ see which of the 15 000 suburbs and towns in Australia are shooting stars with high imminent price-growth potential

➤ discover where the income-generating cash cows are

➤ learn how to find long shots if you are prepared to speculate

➤ discover how these outcomes are generated by the three demand dynamics of the housing market:

 • people

 • purchasing power

 • properties

➤   see how these demand dynamics work together to cause
     price and rent changes.

Many investors think that accurately predicting the property
market is next to impossible. They believe that no-one is clever
enough to pick the best time to buy or sell, because the housing
market seems to behave in strange and unexpected ways. They
rely instead on hearsay, gut feelings or speculation, and, while
a few strike it lucky, most end up with results way below their
expectations.

Such experiences have led many investors to adopt the *buy and
hold* method, also known as *time in the market*. This 'safety first'
strategy is based on the belief that housing prices always rise over
time and that this growth evens out, so it doesn't really matter
where you buy an investment property or whether prices fall for
a year or two, because prices will eventually go up everywhere
and, over time, all areas of the market will eventually achieve the
same rate of price-growth.

This idea is simple and anyone can use it. Some experts take this
notion a step further, by claiming that house prices double in value
every eight or so years. On what basis are such statements made?
They are built on the past performance of the housing market.
Experts promoting the buy and hold theory often produce charts
such as figure 1.1, showing that house prices did indeed double
in price every eight years during the 1970s and 1980s.

You can see why this theory has become so popular. If property
prices double every eight years, you need to do little more than
find a property in your price bracket. The location is not crucial
or even important because, once a property is secured, you only

need to hold and hope. But surely, if we are going to base future housing performance on the past performance of the market, we should first check to see whether our current economic, social and financial conditions are roughly the same as those prevailing during the period we are using for comparison.

Figure 1.1: house prices doubled in value every eight years from 1967 to 1990

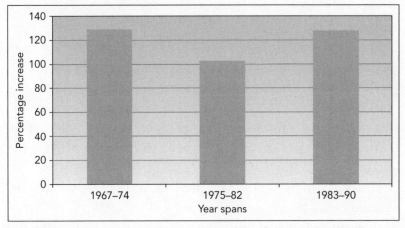

Source: Australian National Library's online Trove facility and Mitchell Library archives.

When we do this, we find that the years from 1970 to 1990 were not typical at all, and certainly nothing like what we are experiencing or likely to experience in the foreseeable future. The 1970s and 1980s witnessed the highest inflation levels in our history; many of those years had double-digit inflation, which was responsible for much of the house price-growth. There was little real price-growth. Those who analyse the past to predict the future ignore this fact completely. Maybe they don't really understand the long-term performance of the housing market at all, or just maybe they promote this theory because it gets them off the hook. Imagine you buy a property and the price starts to fall, and keeps falling for several years. What happens if you complain to whoever advised you? They'll tell you to wait, and assure you that growth will come because it always has in the past. If prices keep falling, they may hope that you'll forget who it was that gave you such bad advice and they'll be off the hook completely.

This focus on past performance is also pushed by project marketers and developers, who use high past price-growth as an indicator of expected growth. 'Get in quick,' they'll tell you, 'or you'll miss out. These properties are selling like hot cakes.' But does past performance guarantee future growth? Some of the best-performing suburbs and towns from 2000 to 2010, where house and unit prices regularly rose by well over 10 per cent per annum, such as the Gold Coast, Mackay, Gladstone, Moranbah and Bowen, suffered massive price falls in the following years. Investors who bought in those towns at the peak of the boom in 2010 then watched in dismay as rental vacancies shot up and prices plummeted by over 50 per cent. Relying on past performance to predict the future is like trying to drive a car by looking through the rear-view mirror. It's a good method to see where you've been, but completely useless at showing you which direction the road ahead is taking.

What we've learned from historical data

The only way that past performance is going to tell us anything at all about the behaviour of the housing market is if we go back not just forty or so years, but far enough to see how it performed through economic booms, recessions and depressions, periods of high and low inflation, war and peace, easy housing finance and no finance, high population growth and low growth. In short, we need to go back in time as far as the data allows us. Luckily some academics have done just that and we can share in what they discovered. Here are their studies:

➤ Stapledon, Nigel, *Long Term Housing Prices in Australia and some Economic Perspectives*. Sydney: University of NSW, 2008.

➤ Eichholtz, Piet, M. A., *A Long Run House Price Index: The Herengracht Index 1628–2008*. Maastricht: Real Estate Economics, 2010.

➤ Lindeman, John, *Mastering the Australian Housing Market*. Melbourne: Wrightbooks, 2011.

➤ Conefrey, Thomas, and Karl Whelan, *Demand and Prices in the US Housing Market*. Dublin: Central Bank of Ireland, 2012.

The Herengracht study analysed nearly four hundred years of house price movements in Amsterdam, while Stapledon's study at the University of NSW researched over one hundred and twenty years of house price changes in Sydney. My own study, published in my previous book, *Mastering the Australian Housing Market*, covered Australian capital city house price movements from 1901 to 2010, while Thomas Conefrey and Karl Whelan analysed the performance of the US housing market from 1968 to 2012. All of these studies came to three very similar and quite amazing conclusions about how the housing market performs over long periods of time. The following pages summarise these findings.

House prices do not double every eight years

Figure 1.2 shows the performance of the Australian capital city housing market since 1903, and it provides a far more sombre picture than that promoted by the buy and hold advocates.

Figure 1.2: house price movements every eight years from 1903 to 2014

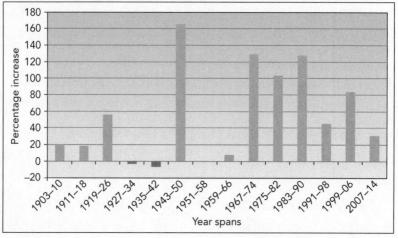

Source: Australian National Library's online Trove facility; Mitchell Library archives.

Since 1903, there have only been four times when house prices doubled in price over eight years. Far more significant is the fact that every other eight-year period has failed to meet this performance benchmark. Not only have there been lengthy periods with little price-growth, house prices actually fell during the 1930s and failed to rise during the 1950s. The price-growth achieved by houses in Australian capital cities every eight years has been about 55 per cent, which means that, on average, it takes 13 years for house prices to double, not eight or even ten.

Unfortunately, even that information is of no use when it comes to predicting the future, because the rate of house price-growth has been highly irregular. It all goes to prove that:

➤ past performance does not predict future performance

➤ there is no housing market cycle or property clock

➤ housing prices have not doubled in price every eight or even ten years

➤ these common assumptions about the housing market's performance are not based on facts, but on assumptions that can be quite misleading.

Luckily for investors, the studies have also identified the cause of this apparent unpredictability.

House prices closely follow the underlying inflation rate

Much of the irregular price-growth of housing is caused by the underlying inflation rate, and it was high inflation that led to the well-touted doubling of house prices every eight years in the 1970s and 1980s. Figure 1.3 (overleaf) demonstrates this correlation, with house prices closely copying the inflation rate, but usually performing slightly better.

Figure 1.3: house price movements mirror the underlying inflation rate

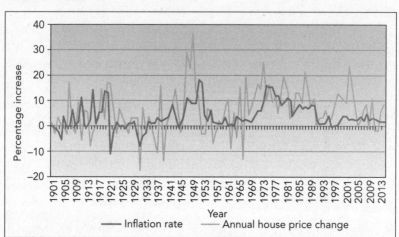

Source: Australian National Library's online Trove facility; Mitchell Library archives; CPI and IRPI data adapted from Data on Request, Australian Bureau of Statistics.

In fact, the only years when house price-growth significantly exceeded the rate of inflation was during the postwar baby boom years of 1947–50, during the years 1970–73 when the baby boomers purchased their own houses, and then again during 1998–2002 when the children of the baby boomers purchased their homes.

The close correlation between house prices and inflation means that the behaviour of the housing market is actually quite predictable, but only when measured at a national level and only over long periods of time. House price-growth in major cities has consistently averaged about 2 per cent per annum above the underlying inflation rate since 1901, but since the end of the Second World War in 1945 this rate has risen to about 3 per cent per year. The cause of the slightly higher growth rate is due to higher demand for housing in capital cities. Our overseas migration rate has been much higher since the war, and most of these new residents prefer to live in cities such as Sydney and Melbourne, resulting in a higher demand for housing than in regional and rural markets.

High demand for city living is unlikely to change anytime in the foreseeable future, giving us a simple rule of thumb to predict price-growth. Over long periods of time, the rate of house price-growth is likely to average about 3 per cent in capital cities plus the underlying rate of inflation. This means that when the annual rate of inflation averages about 2 per cent, a typical investment property is likely to deliver 5 per cent per annum total growth, even though there might be significant price swings from year to year. That is the best that a buy and hold strategy can offer you, because it is based on the actual long term performance of the housing market. If this were all that housing investment provided you might be tempted to buy shares or even gold instead, but it is the third finding about how the housing market performs over long periods of time that is the most significant of all and demonstrates why property investment has the edge over other forms of investment.

Housing prices change in accordance with supply and demand

Some of the years since 1901 witnessed extremely high house price-growth, and others none at all, but the overall performance of all capital cities tends to even out the booms and the busts. When we drill down to individual capital cities as figure 1.4 (overleaf) shows, each year since 2002–03 has produced a different highest price performer.

Figure 1.4: every capital city takes its turn as the highest price performer

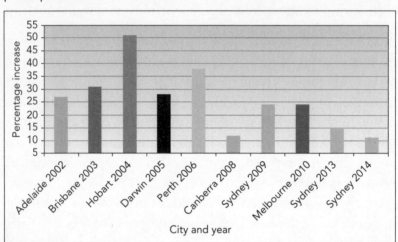

Source: Australian Bureau of Statistics.

Adelaide's house prices rose by over 25 per cent in 2002 and Brisbane's shot up by more than 30 per cent the next year. Not to be outdone, Hobart's house prices rocketed upwards by 50 per cent the following year. In the next ten years, however, there was little price-growth in any of these three capital cities. Sydney, on the other hand, had virtually no house price-growth from 2003 onwards until 2009, and then was the best performer again in 2013 and 2014. But even including these three best performing years, Sydney's total house price-growth from 2002–14 has averaged only 6 per cent per annum, which is still lower than Brisbane, Adelaide, Perth or Hobart over the same time.

Although the annual price-growth of all capital cities was close to the long-term annual average, you can see that each city performed quite differently. This is because price booms are rare and they don't last longer than a year or two, being caused by a sudden increase in buyer demand combined with a shortage of stock available for purchase. While such growth spurts are sweet for investors, they are also short because the high price rises in themselves dampen demand and buyers look elsewhere. They take place in all types of housing markets, at any time — and just as the growth rates between cities can vary hugely, so can the growth in the suburbs of each city.

Some suburbs may be about to boom while others are falling in price. Past performance won't tell you which suburbs are likely to boom, because the conditions that caused price and rent changes in the past are very likely to be different in future. Housing is a commodity and prices will change according to changes in supply and demand. You would think that this simple truth would end the mystery and misinformation out there once and for all, but it hasn't because the housing market doesn't appear to act that way at all.

Housing behaves differently from other commodities because there are in effect two housing markets. About a quarter of the dwellings that make up the property market are investor-owned rented properties. Rental properties and owner-occupied properties can behave very differently from each other in accordance with the changing relationship of demand and supply for properties in each. Demand for housing can flow into either market, so that when housing finance is tight or costly, rental demand increases and the rental market grows in size and value, while if housing finance is cheap and freely available, buyer demand rises and the renter market declines and rents may fall.

Because most suburbs have a combination of both rented and owner-occupied dwellings, prices may rise while rents will fall in some suburbs, although in others both rents and prices may rise or fall or rents can rise yet prices fall. While each of these markets has its own dynamics of demand, they are connected because households move from one to the other, starting out as renters and then usually becoming buyers and sellers. This means that there needs to be a constant supply of properties for them to purchase in the buyer–seller market, and as they leave the renter market there also needs to be a constant supply of new renting households to keep up the rental demand. If you remember that renter demand controls the renter market, while buyers and sellers control the price market, you can unravel the mysteries of why the market behaves as it does and make some meaningful predictions.

The future will not be the same as the past

Some housing market analysts link the housing market's future performance to intangibles such as unaffordability, or to interest rates; national, state or local economic performance; unemployment; infrastructure development; or even to consumer confidence. No matter which of these dynamics (if any) is right, the facts are that the future of our housing market will be very different to its past. No period in history is exactly like any other, and we continually face climatic, social, economic and financial situations that we have never had to deal with before. Analysing these changes helps us to understand why the housing market has performed in the way that it has, but it also teaches us that relying on the recent past to point the way forward is futile.

The difference between making a prediction and a prophecy is to know just how far into the future we can actually see with some certainty. No-one could have accurately predicted the housing market's performance in 2008–09 without also anticipating the intensity of the Millennium drought and the onset of the Global Financial Crisis, along with the subsequent changes in housing finance lending and overseas migration.

This is why long-term prediction is difficult: even with the benefit of the most accurate prediction methods, the further into the future we attempt to predict, the greater the likelihood of unanticipated events that will throw our forecasts into disarray. No matter how good our explanations, short-term forecasts are likely to be more accurate than long-term ones. Luckily the housing market is on our side, because prices and rents can move substantially in relatively short periods of time, and they do so in accordance with easy-to-understand supply and demand principles.

The secret to unlocking the housing market's future is to understand that housing is a commodity that we buy and sell, just like a car, a boat or even an apple. Yet we don't usually think of housing as a commodity, because we normally don't buy our homes as investments but for other reasons. Home provides us with security and comfort, a place to raise a family or retire to. Another reason that we don't think of housing as a commodity is that it doesn't seem to behave like one. Its behaviour often confounds even the most serious analysts, yet if we rely on facts rather than on fables to forecast the future we find that the market behaves in predictable ways.

The housing market suits all types of investors

Understanding how the housing market works enables you to choose the best type of investment because, just as there are different types of investment outcomes, so there are different types of housing markets that can deliver those results. Some suburbs are suited to active 'make it happen' investors who conduct cosmetic or structural renovations for short-term gain, while other areas suit passive 'let it happen' investors who engage in flipping and trading. Some investors want high cash flow and others seek suburbs that have boom price potential. There are even localities with few prospects apart from hearsay or gossip that something big is about to happen, where investors speculate on a 'hope it happens' basis. Because the housing market is a huge jigsaw puzzle with 10 million properties spread over 15 000 suburbs, we need a simple way of putting the pieces together. This way we can categorise all these suburbs into a few groups that offer similar opportunities, risks and likely performance results.

Figure 1.5 divides the 15 000 suburbs into four distinct groups, each of which offers different outcomes for property investors. These groups are called *cash cows, shooting stars, long shots* and *sleepers*. The suburbs in each have certain characteristics in common that identify them, such as:

➤ types of properties

➤ types of renters

➤ price ranges

➤ location.

Figure 1.5: solving the property investment puzzle

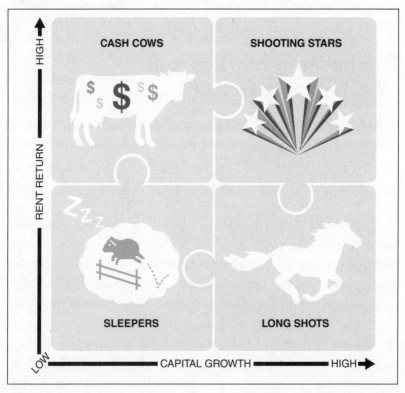

This makes them easy to find and, armed with this knowledge, you will have a much better chance of buying the best possible property in an area where you understand what opportunities are on offer and which hidden dangers may lurk in the background.

Most suburbs are sleepers

Sleeper suburbs form by far the greater number of our capital city and regional town housing markets. This is where median prices and rents move in tune with the overall performance of the market, and the reason this happens is due to the sheer weight of sleeper suburb numbers — it's their rent, price and yield performance that is responsible for the capital city median house and unit price changes we read about. It is therefore essential that investors in such suburbs fully inform themselves about the average performance of the market and the implications for their investments. The key to investment success in sleeper suburbs is being able to read them well enough to pick suburbs for short-term investment just before any price-growth starts, and then sell before it stops.

Some investors get itchy fingers watching the ebb and waiting for the flow of prices in sleeper suburbs, and so they decide to saddle up in search of the elusive long shot suburb where spectacular returns await the more adventurous.

Long shots promise high returns but with high risk

The hope of buying in a town or suburb just before it bursts into spectacular growth is something that appeals to us all. It would truly be like winning a property lottery, because only very few who make investments in long shots ever hit the jackpot. Such investments are based mostly on pure speculation around expectations of increased housing demand in the future, from a new or expanding mine operation, proposed railway line, port or freeway — or from other investors.

Announcements about possible mining or infrastructure development in remote and previously unheralded towns are always accompanied by an increase in house buyers. As a result, the local housing market quickly moves from 'stressed' to 'seller' conditions, and may even boom. But without any genuine housing demand, the number of profit-taking sellers also rises and prices can quickly reach a tipping point if the number of properties on the market approaches the number of buyers. Within a matter of months, prices are stripped down to where they started and even lower, because the number of potential sellers is now far greater than the number of buyers, even though the total number of buyers and sellers during the entire course of the drama is equal.

These price movements have little to do with land's real value, but are all about speculation. For those of you willing to obtain such rewards, remember that the risks are high as well.

Cash cows offer high rental yield and security

Cash cow suburbs are the holy grail of many investors because they provide high rental yield and price stability driven by a constant supply of renters. Rental yield is a function of both the house price and rental rates, as it is the annual rent from a property expressed as a percentage of the purchase price. Because 2 per cent of a property's value is usually spent each year in maintenance, management and expenses, an investment property whose rental yield also covers the loan interest plus the holding costs is said to be *positively geared*. This is because it provides net cash flow back to the investor from the rent. The higher the yield, the better the return; and the highest rental yields usually come from three sources:

➤ Overseas arrivals who move into older, well-established suburbs typified by large ethnic communities and proximity to public transport.

➤ Emerging households (young people leaving home for the first time) who prefer inner urban medium- and high-density living close to recreational and entertainment areas.

➤ Reservoirs of permanent renters: low-income households who live in ex–housing commission dwellings and former holiday homes on the fringes of cities and country towns.

Cash cow suburbs suit investors with fairly modest buying price ranges whose aim is positive cash flow along with the security of price-growth over time. The main risks come from over-development, particularly in inner urban unit precincts, and reduction in the migrant intake due to changes in government policy.

It is also important to determine where overseas arrivals are likely to come from in the future, as this will play a large part in choosing locations where these groups prefer to live until they become established and buy homes of their own. The easiest way to find cash cow suburbs is their shared characteristics of high rental yield and rental demand. Out of all the suburbs and towns in Australia, less than half usually have short-term rent growth potential and, of these, just half again have long-term price stability. It's even more difficult to isolate those suburbs where there are properties that can generate a positive cash flow from day one.

The issue that investors have to face is that the suburbs often featuring in high rental yield lists are there for the wrong reasons. Rental yield is the amount of rent received in a year expressed as a percentage of the purchase price, so if prices fall, it pushes the rental yield up. The rental yield may even rise enough for the suburb to feature as a 'high rental yield' performer, even though this has been caused by falling prices rather than by rising rents. Indeed, some of these suburbs can have abysmal rental vacancy rates. Yet even though there are only a few hundred cash cow suburbs they are not hard to find, because the percentage of renters is well above the national average, housing prices in the suburb are stable and the rental yield is attractive. If the numbers add up, you may well have found your own cash cow suburb.

Shooting stars provide both high rent and price-growth

When the sleeper, long shot and cash cow suburbs are removed from further consideration we are left with something special: the shooting stars, which are investment areas that have high price-growth potential, high rent-growth forecasts and high rental yield. The number of potential candidates diminishes rapidly as we discard suburbs that don't meet all these criteria. Due to the high risk and performance volatility of mining towns you won't find shooting stars there, nor are they in the attendant dormitory towns, ports and processing centres. The attraction of shooting star suburbs for investors is enhanced by the usually low median buying price, normally far less than the median price for the state as a whole, which leaves plenty of room for price-growth. They tend to be located in areas of high population growth with high rental demand and local housing shortages.

The three dynamics of housing markets

Shooting star, cash cow and long shot suburbs are defined by the households moving into them and whether they rent or buy, creating shortages in the process. These changes are called the *dynamics of housing markets*, which simply means the causes of price or rent changes. So to identify the individual investment prospects of any suburb, we need to understand its dynamics.

Knowing how the dynamics of any housing market operates will remove a great deal of uncertainty from your property investment decisions because they reveal the reasons why prices and rents are likely to rise or fall. The good news is that there are only three key housing market dynamics that you need to understand and track to make accurate predictions:

➤ people

➤ purchasing power

➤ properties.

The bad news is that they are so little understood that they seem to be secrets, zealously guarded by the few who know their predictive power. Let's uncover these property prediction secrets and discover how to use them — to see:

➤ how people create housing demand

➤ why purchasing power turns this demand into rentals or purchases

➤ how local shortages or surpluses of properties then result in housing price and rent changes.

One of the reasons that these three property prediction secrets are so little understood is that they always work together to create price and rent changes. Relying on just one in isolation, such as high population growth, or the availability of cheap and easy finance, or a local housing shortage, to predict future performance is flawed, yet many property market predictions are made this way. Because such predictions often fail, they may leave us thinking that the housing market behaves erratically or even illogically and that its current performance is no exception. To discover what is causing seemingly illogical market behaviour and what the likely outcome will be, we need to see how the three key dynamics — people, purchasing power and properties — work together.

People create demand for housing

We all need a place to live, so every new household increases our overall housing demand by one. Figure 1.6 shows the annual change in our population that has occurred since Federation in 1901.

Figure 1.6: Australia's population has always been growing

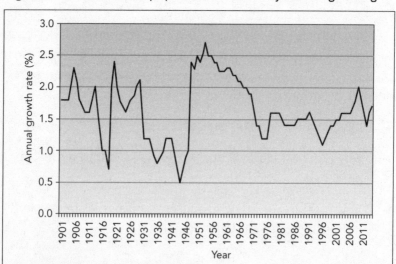

Source: Australian Bureau of Statistics.

The most significant fact is that it has always been growing, even during the darkest years of war, recession or depression. From its lowest annual growth rate of 0.5 per cent in 1944, our population grew by a record 2.7 per cent just a few years later in 1953. Not only has this created a more or less constant shortage of housing, the shortage has been greater in our capital cities, where most of us have preferred to live.

This pressure on housing in capital cities has been worsened by a constant drift to cities by people from the country. In fact, existing households moving from one location to another have a far greater effect on housing markets because every household moving into a suburb increases the demand for a dwelling by one, while at the same time increasing the supply by one in the suburb the household has moved out of. Moreover, the numbers of existing households who move each year is far greater than the numbers of new households, so they have a far bigger impact on local housing markets.

While this movement changes the demand and supply balance wherever it occurs, it is the type of households who are moving into and out of areas that directly affects prices or rents, as well as the number of investors who buy and sell, but don't actually live in the houses or units that they own. Table 1.1 (overleaf) shows the various households who buy and sell properties and the types of housing markets that they create.

Table 1.1: the main types of buyer and seller markets

Type of market	Total households	Average stay	Typical family types	Location of houses	Location of units
First home buyers	1 000 000	4 years	Ex-renters	Outer suburbs	Transport corridors
Moving and improving upgraders	4 000 000	10–30 years	Families with children	Established suburbs	Beaches, bays and views
Retirees	1 000 000	Rest of life	Older households	Coastal towns and retreats	Recreational resorts
Renters	There are about 2 500 000 private investor–owned properties as well as about 500 000 government-owned properties, also known as public housing.				

The four main buyer and seller groups are:

➤ first-home buyers

➤ people upgrading to a bigger home or a better location

➤ retirees making their final purchase

➤ housing market investors.

First home buyers usually buy in the same city where they have been renting, but not the same suburb. They may have been renting an inner urban unit close to recreation and employment, but can only afford to buy an outer suburban house or unit in a growth corridor in a less-than-perfect area. After several years in their first home, most owner-occupiers usually decide it's time to move either to a bigger home in the same location, or to a better location. They hardly ever upgrade to another city because of family, employment and social ties, so the demand they create when they move is concentrated in well-established locations with good facilities and services in the same city and in their purchasing price ranges, which are generally around the median price for the capital city.

After one or two such upgrading moves, the average family does not move again for about 25 years or so, providing the well-established suburbs where they live with the greatest price stability of all types of housing markets. The final move a buyer and seller family makes is when the children have grown up and left and the family home is too big, requires too much maintenance and possibly also represents their greatest asset. The choice of a retirement location is ultimately determined by the nature and location of the new area, the relative purchase price compared to the sale price of the family home and its proximity to the children and grandchildren.

These three types of owner-occupier types of markets make up nearly all of the sleeper suburbs covered earlier in this chapter. So where are the shooting star, long shots and cash cows? They are located in the last group of buyer and seller markets — in those suburbs where investors own most of the properties.

Investors form the second-largest group of buyers and sellers but don't live in their properties. They are motivated purely by profit, can buy and sell without moving and do so more often than other buyers and sellers, but they also create accommodation for renters and so we need to consider the housing markets where they buy and sell properties differently to owner-occupier markets — as the four types of renter markets shown in table 1.2.

Table 1.2: the main types of renter markets

Type of market	Total households	Average stay	Typical family types	Location of houses	Location of units
Permanent private renters	500 000	Permanently	Low incomes, single-parent families	Ex–housing commission, ex–holiday homes, rural outskirts	Older unit enclaves
Overseas arrivals	1 500 000	4 years	Permanent arrivals from overseas	Ethnic enclaves in affordable rental suburbs	Ethnic enclaves near services and facilities
New households	600 000	2 years	Young households leaving home	Established inner suburbs	Inner urban areas with services and facilities
Opportunity seekers	400 000	1 year or less	Singles, groups	Mining, tourist towns, dormitory towns	Mining, tourist towns, dormitory towns

Permanent private renter markets offer high yields and low risk and many form cash cow suburbs, but because of their low prices the opportunity for capital growth is diminished. Temporary renter markets cross a wide spectrum of prices and offer great variations in growth potential and rental yield as well as presenting varying degrees of risk depending entirely on the types of renters moving into and out of an area. They may be inner urban high rise precincts favoured by new younger households looking for quality lifestyle, modern facilities and proximity to entertainment and employment, or older suburbs where recent arrivals from overseas can find rental accommodation near ethnically similar neighbours, schools, shops and religious institutions. They may be new mining towns or tourist resorts where the people seeking employment are renters with no intention to buy a property, because they will only stay while the opportunities last.

Every type of housing market performs differently as time goes by — sometimes first home buyers lead a growth charge, at other times it may be retirees. Investors may buy into high rental demand areas such as mining towns or inner urban unit precincts and create growth and then depart again if rental demand dries up. On the other hand, there are some regions and localities where populations are falling. Decreasing populations in Australia are caused by people moving to another state, or another area within the same state; such movements may be hidden by commonly used statistics. Figure 1.7 shows that while Tasmania's two largest cities, Hobart and Launceston, maintain a healthy population growth rate, the rest of the state is falling in population.

Figure 1.7: Tasmania's annual rural population drain

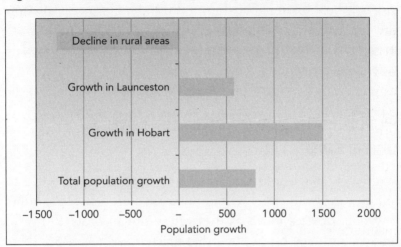

Source: Australian Bureau of Statistics.

Thousands of younger Tasmanians leave the state each year, seeking better employment, educational, recreational and social opportunities. This is causing a population decline in rural Tasmania that is hidden because, at the same time, an almost equal number of older people move from the mainland looking for affordable retirement options or lifestyle changes. Although young people leave empty nests behind rather than empty houses and interstate arrivals need housing immediately, the effect is more dramatic on the housing market in rural areas because the younger people leaving are not being replaced.

Tasmanian rural towns such as Zeehan, Roseberry and Queenstown often feature in free reports because they periodically generate the highest rental yields of any Australian housing market, but be warned: younger people are deserting those towns, leaving behind ageing populations, high rental vacancies, falling house prices and a rising number of derelict and deserted homes. This is why you need to understand the type of housing market that predominates in any area where you may be thinking of buying an investment property and how the demand is changing — that is, what types of households are moving in and which are leaving — as this helps you to estimate whether prices and rents may change.

Purchasing power creates buyers or renters

When new households are formed or move from one area to another, they will either rent or purchase a property. First home buyers borrow as much as they can afford in order to live in an area and type of dwelling that meets their needs, but there is usually some trade-off involved, because the amount they can borrow as well as the repayment commitments are limited by lenders. Upgraders will have some equity, may have higher incomes and the interest rate may have shifted in their favour over time, so they can afford to move to a bigger dwelling, or a better area by increasing the borrowed amount. Over time, they may even be able to use their equity to reduce the amount financed and still be able to upgrade. In fact, most retirees will use their equity to buy a suitable retirement home, retire their debts and still have a nest egg left over for the future. Investors will either buy for capital growth, in which case they will borrow most of the purchase price to leverage their investment, or buy for cash flow, in which case they will borrow as little as possible and provide rental accommodation.

Just as not all buyers need finance, not all renters intend to buy. The crucial point here is that most aspiring home buyers will purchase their first home in a different suburb to where they live. A young couple renting a high-rise unit in inner Sydney or Melbourne is highly likely to buy their first home in an affordable outer suburb, where they intend to start or expand their family.

Overseas arrivals will rent in affordable middle distance suburbs until they are sufficiently well settled to buy their own home, and this is likely to be a statement of their successful establishment in a new country. This means that as new households and overseas arrivals change from renters to purchasers, they reduce the demand for rentals in the suburbs they leave and increase the demand for purchased homes in the areas they move to. There are, however, two groups of renters whose primary aim is not to purchase a home — at least not directly. They are the 500 000 permanently renting households on low incomes in ex–housing commission and holiday home areas. Although they are located on the outskirts of our major cities, they may also rent older, less desirable units in urban areas as well as older houses in country towns. The other group are the opportunity-seeking renters, looking for high income employment in mining towns, casual employment and holiday lifestyles in tourist resorts or education in university towns. Although they have no immediate intention to purchase homes of their own, and certainly not in the towns where they are renting, they are a highly mobile group of renters and control the fortunes of investors who buy properties in such areas. It is their demand for accommodation or lack of it that sets the boom or bust sequence in motion.

We have seen that the continual rise in our population has led to a more or less constant shortage of housing, especially in capital cities, but this does not automatically lead to a rise in housing prices, because some households cannot afford to buy a home, or don't want to. Figure 1.8 (overleaf) shows how this has played out since 1901, with rents rising strongly during periods such as the Great Depression in the early 1930s, when housing finance was simply not available, or during the early 1950s when large numbers of postwar overseas arrivals were forced to rent for several years until they were settled.

Figure 1.8: either house prices or rents have always been rising

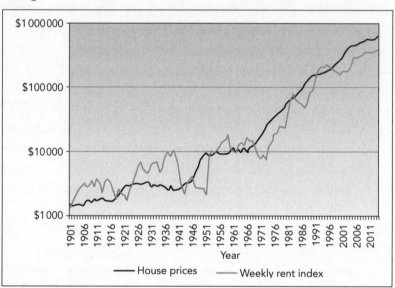

Source: Australian National Library's online Trove facility; Mitchell Library archives.

At other times, such as the immediate postwar years of 1919 to 1921 and 1946 to 1951, house prices rose strongly as soldiers arrived back home from years of service, keen to start families and buy homes with generous government war service home loan assistance. Figure 1.8 shows how rents actually fell in those years as new households left rental accommodation to move into new suburban homes they were buying.

Demand and supply changes in properties lead to shortages or surpluses

Because of the issues with collecting timely population movement data and housing finance data for areas smaller than capital cities and states, some predictive systems resort to other methods of trying to estimate demand, such as time on market, vendor discounting, rental yield, or even online search interest ratios, none of which may be accurate or even appropriate. How then can we measure the number of people moving into or out of a suburb and determine whether they are renters or owners?

We can simply do this by measuring the effect they have on the housing market. If people move into a suburb and buy properties, the numbers of property sales rise and the number of properties for sale goes down. If they move out, the number of property sales falls but the number of properties for sale goes up. This will only lead to a rise in property prices if the number of potential buyers climbs above the number of properties for sale. In other words, if there is a shortage of properties available for purchase, and potential purchasers start to compete with each other to buy. So if the number of buyers rises but there are plenty of properties for sale on the market, prices will not go up. This is the law of supply and demand and it works in the property market just as it does with any other commodity. It also means that a fall in sales will not necessarily lead to a fall in price, unless the number of properties for sale, that is the supply, is more than the demand.

Some movers don't buy; they rent. But the same rules apply, in that if the number of potential renters rises above the number of rental vacancies, rents are likely to rise as prospective tenants compete with each other. On the other hand, if rental demand drops and results in a rise in rental vacancies, investors trying to let their properties will compete with each for tenants and rents will fall.

It would seem, then, that all we have to do is determine where households are likely to move in future, and whether they are likely to purchase or rent, and we can accurately predict housing demand in those areas. We can estimate whether this could lead to a shortage or surplus of properties and even forecast the probable changes in prices and rents.

In fact there are some predictive systems in the market that attempt just this task, but there are some fundamental issues with this approach. First, housing data such as the number of renters, number of properties, even number of residents in a suburb is only gathered every five years by the Bureau of Statistics in the Census of Population and Housing. More frequent updates are trend estimates and not provided at suburb level, so the data being used in these predictive systems is not current, and could be up to six years out of date. Second, the only effective 'rent or buy' statistic is Housing Finance, but although this is provided monthly by the Bureau of Statistics, it does not drill down below capital city and states, so we don't know where owner-occupiers or investors are buying properties. In addition, housing finance data doesn't give us any information at all about purchasers who don't need finance, such as retirees.

It is as if there are two housing markets in any suburb: one for renters and another for buyers and sellers. They can behave very differently, but it will always be the supply and demand situation in each that determines whether rents or prices will rise or fall.

This first key has unlocked the mysteries of how the housing market works and demonstrated the importance of looking forward rather than backwards. We have solved the investor puzzle and revealed the three dynamics of the housing market, to show you how they lead to price and rent changes. The next key shows you how to easily measure the current state of any housing market and predict its likely price and rent performance.

Key 2

Find areas with the best growth potential

The previous key showed you how the housing market works and we revealed the three dynamics of the housing market: people, purchasing power and properties. This key shows you how to:

➤ easily and quickly read the housing market in a suburb, including:

- how to tell if overdevelopment is likely
- whether it is a good idea to speculate in a particular area

➤ predict the likely price performance of any suburb or town anywhere in Australia.

No housing market prediction can be 100 per cent correct in practice because random events may intervene and change the dynamics in unexpected ways. The further ahead a forecast is made, the more likely it is that such events will occur, so predictions made for three or more years into the future often end up being based on prophecy rather than fact.

Nevertheless, the three housing market dynamics of population, purchasing power and properties are the constants operating in the housing market that work together to cause price and rent movements. They are easily tracked, so that you can check the accuracy of any housing market prediction.

We have seen that it is impossible to obtain accurate indications of population and housing finance changes at suburb level, simply because no-one measures them. Some reports show population or income growth from one census to the next as part of their selection basis for suburbs, meaning that they are relying on growth figures from, for example, 2006 to 2011, which is almost ancient history. Many suburbs, especially those in inner urban renewal precincts and outer suburban areas in our major cities, have undergone significant demographic changes since then. Be wary of any reports that rely on census data, or even worse, do not even reveal the sources of their demographic data.

Other researchers and analysts go through contortions to try to estimate where people are moving and whether they will rent or buy. The types of statistics that they look at include:

➤ employment changes

➤ economic changes

➤ affordability

➤ income levels

➤ cost of finance

➤ consumer confidence.

The issue is that while all of these may have some general effect on the housing market, none of them can be assessed at suburb level.

This forces some experts to dig deeper and look at housing market indicators or measurements such as:

➤ dwelling approvals

➤ building commencements

➤ stock on market

➤ vendor discounting

➤ time on market

➤ auction clearance rates

➤ hold time between sales

➤ rental yields

➤ rental vacancy rates

➤ online search ratios

➤ keyword trawls

➤ listings to stock ratios

➤ median sale price movements.

While some of these figures may well provide useful information about a local housing market, they are hard to obtain and difficult to understand. Many are based on samples and others are simply unreliable. Taken as a whole they are even likely to provide completely contradictory conclusions. The only accurate way to measure where people are moving and whether they are buying, selling or renting, is by watching their effect on the:

➤ number of property sales

➤ properties listed for sale

➤ rental vacancies

in any suburb or town.

Predict short-term price and rent changes

Housing prices are subject to the same laws of supply and demand as other commodities, and they can change quite dramatically at suburb level in response to rises and falls in potential buyer and seller numbers. In particular we can estimate when and where dramatic growth spurts, known as *booms*, are likely, and be ready to make a purchase decision. Because such growth is sweet but short, only a small percentage of the 15000 housing market suburbs have boom potential at any one time, but by buying in those suburbs and then selling before the growth stops, investors can make significantly higher returns than those who 'hold and hope', even with the high entry and exit costs that such short-term investments tend to incur. This makes it important for you to know both the current type of market in a suburb as well as how it is predicted to perform in the future. To make this easy, we can describe the current type of house or unit market in any suburb as one of the five possible types shown in table 2.1.

Table 2.1: the five types of house or unit markets

◄ Prices falling	No change	Prices rising ►
Stressed Buyer	Neutral	Seller Boom

Note: Every suburb has one of these types of house or unit markets.

Source: Adapted from Property Power Database, Property Power Partners.

Stressed markets

Stressed markets are suburbs with many potential sellers and few intending buyers. Prices are likely to be falling by more than 10 per cent per annum and changes tend to take several years to occur because of the large surplus of properties in the market waiting to be sold. If the prediction is for stressed market conditions to continue, prices will keep falling by more than 10 per cent per annum until and if the market eventually changes to a buyer market.

Buyer markets

Buyer markets are suburbs where there are more potential sellers than intending buyers and there's a tendency for prices to fall by 10 per cent or less per annum. Due to the surplus of properties listed for sale on the market, these markets are slow-moving and the change to a neutral or stressed market can take up to a year or more to occur.

Neutral markets

Neutral markets are suburbs where the numbers of potential sellers and intending buyers is equally balanced; there is little opportunity for anything other than small price falls or rises to occur while such conditions continue. It usually takes from six months to a year for neutral markets to change to buyer or seller markets.

Seller markets

Seller markets are suburbs with fewer potential sellers than intending buyers and there is continual pressure on prices to rise, although the rise is usually 10 per cent per annum or less. Because of the low numbers of properties listed for sale on the market, these suburbs can change to boom markets or change back to neutral markets in six months or less if conditions change.

Boom markets

Boom markets are suburbs with few potential sellers and many intending buyers. Prices are likely to be rising by more than 10 per cent per annum and will continue to rise at this rate if the prediction is for boom conditions to continue. Because there are typically few properties listed for sale in such suburbs, they have the most price volatility and can revert to seller markets within three months if buyer demand decreases.

The five types of housing markets shown in table 2.1 (on p. 36) can apply either to house or to unit markets, but you should never assume that a suburb's houses and units have the same types of markets, as they can be very different. A suburb may simultaneously have a shortage of houses on the market and a surplus of units listed for sale and they could be trending in different directions. To take this snapshot in time of the current type of housing market, we simply look up the ratio of annual sales as published in the Databank in *Australian Property Investor* magazine for houses or units in the suburb in which we are interested, and then look up the number of current online listings for house or units for sale in that suburb.

Using the ratios shown in table 2.2 you can easily check the current state of any suburb's housing market by comparing the total number of sales in the last year for houses or units to the total number of houses or units currently listed for sale in that suburb.

Table 2.2: what the annual sales and current listings totals tell us

Four or more times current listings as annual sales	Three or less times current listings as annual sales	About the same number of current listings as annual sales	Ten or less times annual sales as current listings	Eleven or more times annual sales as current listings
Stressed	Buyer	Neutral	Seller	Boom

Source: Adapted from Property Power Database, Property Power Partners.

In other words, a suburb with 20 house sales in the last year and 40 houses currently listed for sale on the market is a buyer market, while a suburb with 20 houses sold in the last year and 20 current house listings is a neutral market and a suburb with 40 house sales in the last year and only three houses currently listed for sale is a boom market.

If your selected suburb is a buyer or stressed market, it's going to take a large movement of new households into the suburb to take up the surplus before any price rise can occur, and this could take years. During all this time, housing prices will probably continue to fall, so that any future rise first needs to claw back previous losses. The bigger the ratio of current listings to annual sales, the longer this will take. On the other hand, if your selected suburb is a seller or boom market, prices are already rising because there are stock shortages and the only question is whether you can find a property that meets your investment criteria, is priced at fair market value or lower, and whether the demand will continue to outpace supply so that prices continue to rise.

While the listings data is current when you obtain it online, the reason I use *Australian Property Investor* magazine's published annual sales for houses or units is that this information is easy for you to find and the ratios have already been put to work, as this is published data that is three months old by the time you use it. The time lag doesn't really matter, because the published annual sales figure in the magazine is updated each month, with the oldest month's sales being subtracted and the new month's sales added to the annual figure. This simple analysis is like a snapshot, frozen in time, of the state of the house or unit market when you do it. But if you do this analysis every month when you receive your *Australian Property Investor* magazine, you start to build up a series of snapshots of the same suburb. This is what statisticians call a *trend*, and using trends to predict the future is one of most accurate forecasting methods there is. Table 2.3 shows how the changing annual sales and current listings trends indicate which way a market is moving.

Table 2.3: what the changing annual sales and current listings trends tell us

Stressed	Buyer	Neutral	Seller	Boom
←	Fewer sales		More sales	→
←	More listings		Fewer listings	→

Source: Adapted from Property Power Database, Property Power Partners.

Not every suburb will end up as a stressed or boom type of market. In Key 1 I explain how most suburbs are sleepers and only occasionally burst into high price-growth, with some even becoming shooting stars. It takes longer for suburbs to move from stressed or buyer conditions, because there are large numbers of stock on the market waiting to be sold. At the other end of the scale, things can move quickly, because there are few properties listed for sale.

By trending the sales and listings figures each month you may well find your own shooting star suburb before anyone else, because those figures are the only accurate leading price change indicators at suburb level and reflect the true changing nature of supply and demand. The best time to buy is in a neutral market where the suburb is moving into seller or boom market conditions. You can continue to hold your investment property in the expectation of continued growth as long as the suburb's market position does not worsen.

You can update your research every month, but the most important thing is to be consistent; use the same data sources and don't set yourself a research schedule that proves too time consuming and ultimately causes you to put off the whole process. By also recording the median sale price you will see how the price changes take effect — bearing in mind that this is a lagging indicator.

What I mean by lagging is, when a property is sold, it takes several months before settlement occurs, at which time the details are sent to the government department or agency responsible for recording the transfer from one owner to another. This information is purchased by data providers, who then calculate the new median sale price for each suburb based on the number of sales that took place in each preceding month. This data is provided to property investment magazines, and then it takes several more months before the data is published, because of the time required to produce, print and then distribute the magazines. This is why published sale price data is already several months old when you receive it; it is providing information about the median sale price of properties sold even earlier.

How to generate your own housing market forecasts

The annual sales and median price data you need is published in *Australian Property Investor* magazine, and real time listings data, that is, number of houses for sale, can be collected from any major property listing site. Even if the listing site does not show all available data, your aim is to pick up trends — and a sizable sample will do this for you. Also be aware that each site has different ways of assembling and displaying the data, so make sure that you are obtaining only the data you require for the type of properties and suburb that you are interested in and assemble your housing research data in a table or spreadsheet such as table 2.4.

Table 2.4: tracking the market in a suburb

Suburb name			Houses or units		
Month	Current listings	Published annual sales	Published median sale price	Ratio	Type of market
July 2015	20	20	$350 000	1 to 1	Neutral

Because property investment magazines are published monthly, it is easiest to update your spreadsheet at the same time each month when you receive the magazine. Remember that the two numbers you are obtaining are quite different — the number of listings (houses for sale) is a one-off snapshot of the total number of houses or units advertised for sale at the time you look this up, so it's real-time data, while the annual sales (number sold) shown in the back of the magazine is the annual sales total, updated monthly so it provides a demand trend.

When you update the spreadsheet each month it enables you to calculate the ratio of listings to sales (which is the ratio of supply to demand) and to see how this is trending. This does not need to be extremely accurate, as long as you can track the trend (if there is one). For example, if listings are rising and the annual sales total is falling, then the trend is worsening.

Read the trends

Remember that it is not changes in the number of sales and listings that causes price changes, but changes in their relationship, or the ratio between them that leads to such movements. There are some traps that you can easily fall into. For example, though sales may be rising as shown in figure 2.1, if listings are also rising at the same rate then the difference between them does not alter. This means that prices will keep rising at the same rate as they currently are.

Figure 2.1: both listings and sales increasing

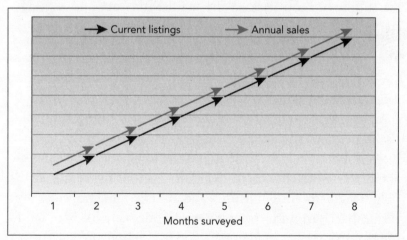

If the numbers of sales and listings are both declining, as shown in figure 2.2 (overleaf), it indicates that price falls will continue at the current rate until the dynamics eventually change.

Figure 2.2: both listings and sales decreasing

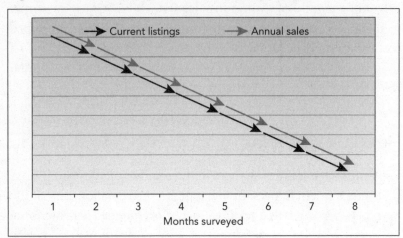

These types of markets illustrate the danger of relying on either sales or listings but not both, because even when sales are rising, prices may still fall if the rate of supply grows faster than demand — and when sales are falling, prices may still rise when the supply of properties on the market runs out and shortages start to occur.

The aim of forecasting is to predict when and which way prices are likely to change, and this can only happen when the *tipping point* is reached, which is when the market moves into surplus or shortage caused by a drop in demand and/or rise in supply, or rise in demand and/or fall in supply. The tipping point is when the number of current listings and the total of annual sales are about the same (indicated in figure 2.3 and figure 2.4 at the point where the current listings and annual sales lines cross over each other). From this point onwards, prices are likely to fall in the example shown in figure 2.3 and to rise in figure 2.4.

Figure 2.3: listings increasing and sales decreasing

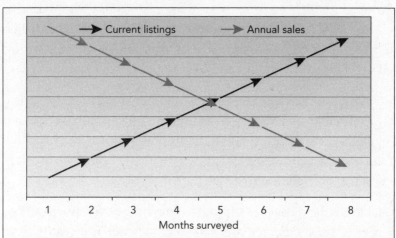

Figure 2.4: listings decreasing and sales increasing

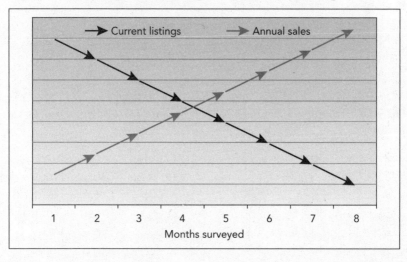

This simple method of housing market price prediction is highly accurate because it always looks forward, with the changes in listings and sales indicating the direction of likely price changes. The greater the difference between listings and sales, the higher the likely amount of price change, possibly even resulting in stressed or boom market conditions. Though not every suburb will move through all the various types of housing markets, the trend shows you which way the local market is heading and, because published sale prices lag by up to six months (as explained earlier in this chapter), you will have a head start when making a buy or sell decision based on the ratio of current listings to annual sales.

As a suburb moves from one type of market to another, the short-term sales and listings trends indicate the best time to consider buying a house or unit. Once the tipping point is reached, the trend will then show you which way the market (and the median sale price) is likely to move.

In table 2.5 the monthly sales and listings in the NSW town of Hay were recorded and tracked over a ten-month period from early 2014.

Table 2.5: example of how the type of market in a suburb changes

Suburb name	Hay		Houses or units	Houses	
Month	Current listings	Published annual sales	Published median sale price	Ratio	Type of market
1	80	40	$90 000	2 to 1	Buyer
2	70	45	$90 000	2 to 1	Buyer
3	60	55	$90 000	1 to 1	Neutral
4	70	70	$90 000	1 to 1	Neutral
5	60	80	$90 000	1 to 1	Neutral
6	50	100	$100 000	1 to 2	Seller
7	40	120	$120 000	1 to 3	Seller
8	25	125	$130 000	1 to 5	Seller
9	20	140	$160 000	1 to 7	Seller
10	12	140	$180 000	1 to 11	Boom

Source: Property Power Database, Property Power Partners.

By month four or five, an investor would notice that the sales were trending upwards and listings downwards each month and that it was highly likely to result in seller market conditions. Buying at this time the investor could secure a median-priced property for about $90 000 and within another five months, because the market went from seller to boom conditions, the house price doubled.

Because the median sale price is a lagging indicator, further house price rises would be likely and the investor could simply keep an eye on the ratio of listings to annual sales to estimate when it might be time to sell. Not every suburb or town will provide the same results as Hay did, but the value of this simple forecasting system is that it can enable you to compare the potential performance of different areas and also to investigate the actual causes of demand if the numbers start to change dramatically.

In Hay, for example it was clear from month four that something was on, and some on-the-ground research revealed that the largest cotton gin in the southern hemisphere was about to be constructed there, which was likely to cause a huge rise in housing demand. The house market boomed and not only did prices more than double, but rents rose dramatically as well. Using this simple tracking system, an investor could have purchased in Hay just before prices rose and made a significant profit, because the changing relationship between listings and sales indicates which way the market is likely to move in the short term.

This is how listings and sales play their part in alerting you to changes in trends and their likely impact on the local housing market. If you use a similar tracking system, over time you should notice a relationship between the listings and the monthly sales and median sale price and you should become an accurate forecaster of imminent price changes. This forecasting methodology has been proven to be about 90 per cent accurate, which begs the question: why is it not 100 per cent accurate? After all, it is firmly based on the foundations and immutable laws of supply and demand. The answer to this question is that both supply and demand can be fiddled with in ways that are peculiar to the housing market and, by understanding how to recognise such situations before they occur, your forecasting should be even more accurate.

The dangers of overdevelopment

One of the unforeseen dangers that housing investors must deal with is the prospect of overdevelopment. While many investors might view further development in an area as a good outcome, leading to improved amenities and facilities and generating higher prices, the reality is that high-density unit development or new subdivisions can have very different outcomes. It depends on who these dwellings are marketed to, as well as their price and quality compared to existing stock in the area.

New developments marketed to owner-occupiers can lead to the rejuvenation of entire suburbs if the new stock is substantially superior to existing stock, such as in the refurbishment of older inner suburbs in major cities. On the other hand, they can cause a deterioration in prices if the new stock is inferior, such as loft and studio apartments in inner urban areas, or single-bedroom retirement villas in coastal resorts. New developments marketed off the plan to investors can lead to an oversupply of rental properties if the rate of new rental stock on the market exceeds the rate of demand. This may not be apparent while rental guarantees are provided by the project marketers, but once the rental oversupply emerges it leads to the potential for both rent and price falls as frustrated and even desperate investors try to sell, often many at the same time.

How to check for potential overdevelopment

You need to check the numbers to see whether there is any possibility of an oversupply, which can easily occur due to a number of factors:

➤ Developers often work without the benefit of reliable predictive data about housing demand and so tend to rely on past performance to select the best areas for new housing and use recent price and rent growth to promote their developments to investors.

➤ It takes housing developers years to work their way through the various development stages, so rental demand in a mining town or dormitory town may be falling just as a supply of new housing comes on the market.

➤ Many of these developments are sold off the plan, before work has been completed or even commenced, so that the properties may not actually be occupied for several years after they have been purchased, by which time the market may have drastically changed.

Examples such as the collapse of the Gold Coast high-density unit market from 2008 onwards show us that while it is essential to analyse and estimate potential demand, forecasting future supply is equally important.

Because of these factors, you should ensure that your selected suburb is not a candidate for overdevelopment by checking its development potential for land subdivision, house and land sales and medium- or high-rise unit development using these three research techniques:

➤ *Drive or walk around the suburb.* Check whether there are large vacant unused land areas, roads ending abruptly that are obviously intended to go further in the future, vacant shopping strips on main roads with no 'to let' signs or blocks or groups of vacant, even derelict terraces or houses in an area with medium- to high-rise units. These are all signs that developers own the land.

➤ *Check a listing site for new or off-the-plan house or unit listings.* What often initially appears as one listing on the real estate site may reveal a potential development of several hundred units or a land subdivision. Go to the developer's or project marketer's site to see their plans for future development of the project, including the number and type of dwellings proposed and the timeline for both sales and occupation.

➤ *Check with the local council.* Any development applications in the area, the number and type of dwellings proposed and the timeline for both sales and occupation will be available through the council.

If there are significant numbers of new developments underway or proposed in a suburb or locality, you need to check the developer's and project marketer's websites to see:

➤ who they are being marketed to (overseas investors, local investors or owner/occupiers)

➤ the comparative quality of the new stock compared to existing stock (compare listings for new stock to those for existing stock of similar types of housing)

➤ the asking price of these dwellings compared to existing stock in the area.

The lure of property speculation

One of the most enticing carrots that the property market occasionally dangles before us is the promise of huge capital growth, usually associated with exciting news of:

➤ a new railway line

➤ a mine being opened or expanded

➤ a proposed port expansion

➤ a new university

➤ a new hospital.

Prospective housing investors are assured that a boom is imminent and urged to get in before the growth starts. This sort of speculative investment is based on a simple rule that has nothing to do with the demand for accommodation, but on the premise that you need to get in first and then get out first. You can buy properties in some remote or otherwise improbable location at bargain prices well before other less-informed investors find out about the proposed development project that will change everything.

The announcements that lead to such housing market booms are always associated with the development of some new type of infrastructure, so it's worthwhile taking a look at what 'infrastructure' actually is and how it affects housing markets. Infrastructure refers to the freeways, ports, railways and airports that enable communities and industries to operate effectively. Because they are huge undertakings, they can take years to complete. They cause housing booms when they open up areas for development, creating new communities, towns and even cities. This process has a long history, starting as far back as the nineteenth century when our interior was developed. At first, inland ports such as Wilcannia in NSW, Echuca in Victoria and Morgan in South Australia flourished as people and goods travelled along the Murray and Darling rivers. Those ports fell into disuse when the railway age arrived, but this opened up other growth opportunities for investors. Regional railway towns such as Werris Creek and Junee in NSW, Seymour and Shepparton in Victoria and Peterborough in South Australia had their time in the sun as the railways extended into the hinterlands. All these towns experienced similar patterns of property price boom, decline, revival and decay because they relied on the building and maintenance of infrastructure projects to create housing demand.

More recently, we saw a revival of port development in coastal cities such as Port Hedland and Gladstone and the infrastructure boom pattern occurred, as shown in figures 2.5 and 2.6.

Figure 2.5: Port Hedland's housing boom and bust

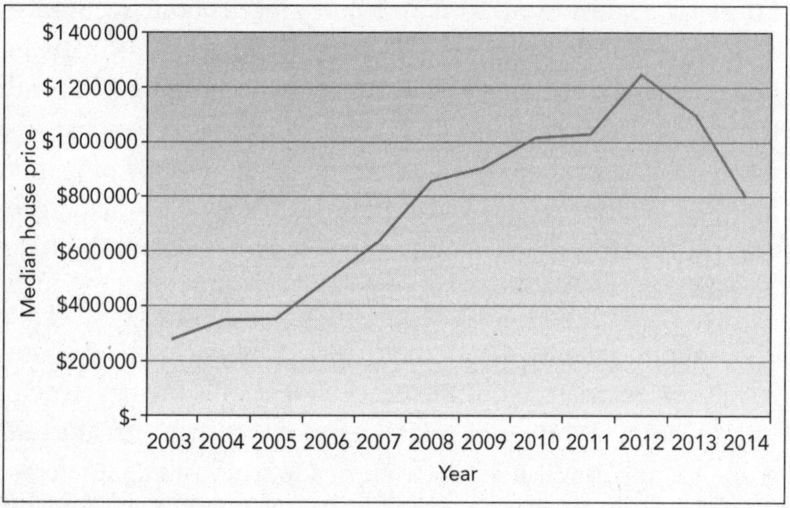

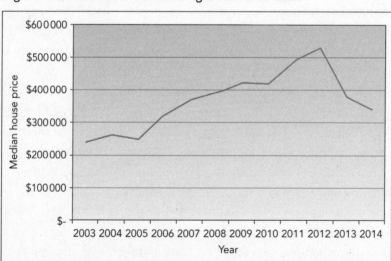

Source: Property Power Database, Property Power Partners.

Figure 2.6: Gladstone's housing boom and bust

Source: Property Power Database, Property Power Partners.

These two markets were often touted as typical infrastructure hotspots and they behaved in a similar fashion over the last ten years. We can see that price-growth in both cities was high from 2005 to 2008 and again in 2011–12, yet before and after these years prices did not grow at all or they fell. These changes reflect the different effects that infrastructure development projects have on housing markets as they move through several stages:

➤ speculation

➤ construction.

Construction phases (the years of highest price-growth shown in figures 2.5 and 2.6) can provide high rents from workers involved in the project, plus price-growth from investors chasing high yields. These are true infrastructure development booms, but before we look at where they will occur and how to obtain the greatest benefit from them, we need to look at the speculative stages of a project first, because this is where investors are most likely to come unstuck.

Speculation

Announcements regarding a new infrastructure project are usually followed by housing price rises, such as the initial lift we see in figures 2.5 and 2.6, but the graphs also show how these first price rises can stall and sometimes fall before a single sod is turned. The rise in housing demand is purely speculative, caused by investors jumping in early to secure low prices. The stakes for loss are high because projects invariably suffer from changes and delays. The history of announcements for new freeways, railways, tunnels, ports or bridges is littered with amendments, delays and abandonments as governments come and go, funds dry up or priorities alter.

A classic example is the Victorian Regional Rail Link, which started as the Fast Rail Project way back in 2000, promising to drastically cut train times from Victoria's three major regional cities. The proposed reduction of travelling time from Geelong to 45 minutes, Ballarat to 60 minutes and Bendigo to 80 minutes was to bring residents in these cities within commuting distance of Melbourne and started a round of property speculation and development based on these outcomes. It was a brilliant concept and promised to revolutionise regional Victoria, but substantial modifications, cutbacks and delays have dramatically changed the vision.

In fact, as figure 2.7 shows, the average annual house price-growth of the three regional cities since the Regional Rail Link project was announced has been lower than that of Melbourne, even despite the hype that surrounded the announcement back in the early 2000s. The general expectation by investors that prices in the three regional cities would boom as a result was never realised.

Figure 2.7: house price-growth in regional Victorian cities and Melbourne

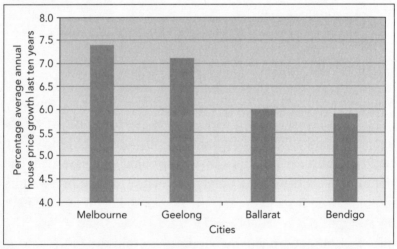

Source: Australian Property Monitors house price data adapted from *Australian Property Investor* Databank.

If we look at the history of Port Hedland's housing market in more detail, we can clearly see the speculative period after the immense high-grade iron ore deposits in the Pilbara were discovered and the intention to mine and export them via Port Hedland was announced. As there was no initial housing shortage, house price rises were slow and irregular and rental demand was slack. The only option for investors wanting to take a profit was to sell to other investors who still expected further price-growth (even though doubts existed that the ore could ever be profitably mined and exported because of its remote and inaccessible location). At this stage, property investment in Port Hedland was purely speculative.

Figure 2.8 shows the lethargic house price-growth that occurred right up until 2003 when China's demand for high-grade Pilbara iron ore changed everything.

Figure 2.8: the stages of Port Hedland's mining boom

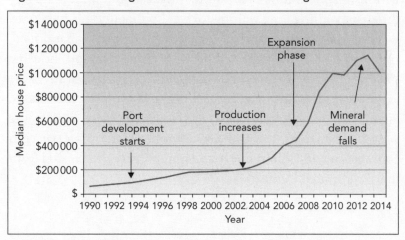

Source: Housing data provided by Australian Property Monitors.

Port Hedland's median house price of $200 000 in 2004 doubled to $400 000 in 2006 when demand was no longer speculative; it was firmly based on a genuine demand for local housing. Investors were able to buy positively geared properties providing a net return from day one due to the extreme shortage of rental accommodation as prices doubled again by 2008, reaching $1 000 000 in 2010. Port Hedland is now in its third stage, which is one of consolidation. Only future demand for iron ore and the ability of Pilbara mines to produce it competitively will stem the otherwise inevitable slide of housing prices.

The investors who did best were those who bought before prices started escalating and then sold to other investors when they had peaked. Such experiences occasionally motivate investors to buy in other potential mining, tourist or infrastructure development locations with the expectation of price-growth that is based purely on speculation. But while they expect a huge growth wave in housing prices and rents, they may instead find something very different, wasting time waiting for wealth that doesn't eventuate. Even worse, when proposed projects are delayed, abandoned, or fail to deliver the expected lift in housing demand, housing prices can fall and sometimes even crash as frustrated investors jostle each other in a rush to sell out and avoid further losses. Figure 2.9 demonstrates how this recently played out in the western Tasmanian town of Zeehan, once a city on a par with Launceston and Hobart due to the immense wealth created from the silver mined in the area.

Figure 2.9: the stages of a speculative mining town (Zeehan, Tasmania)

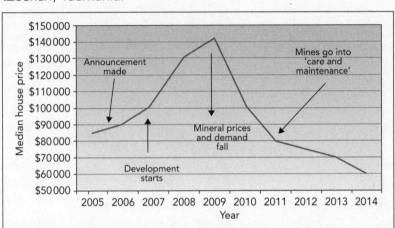

Source: Housing data provided by Australian Property Monitors.

During the mining boom years leading up to the Global Financial Crisis, a number of mining companies announced expansion plans and new mines to develop the remaining nickel, zinc and tin mineral reserves around Zeehan. Speculators rushed in to buy houses in town for under $100000 and prices soon rose to over $130000, with investors expecting housing demand to soar just like in Port Hedland. Sadly, within a year it was all over—the nickel, tin and zinc ores turned out to be of lower quality and quantity than expected, and falling mineral prices and demand put an end to the new mining ventures. House prices in Zeehan fell well below their pre-boom levels.

The very different examples of Port Hedland and Zeehan serve to illustrate that there are two reasons growth can occur in any housing market. The first is speculative demand from investors who compete against each other to buy properties in the expectation of further growth. The second is genuine demand for accommodation, which can be generated directly by owner-occupiers or indirectly by renters, who drive up rents and attract investors in the process.

Any growth in housing prices created by a new mine, infrastructure project or tourist resort before actual accommodation shortages occur is pure speculation. The rise in buyer demand can lead to price booms that have nothing to do with the actual demand for homes to live in. All speculative booms can become price bubbles that will burst unless there is a real increase in demand for local accommodation. Even when some new project is completed, the effect on housing prices may be very different to what investors expect, and in some cases there may be no appreciable effect at all.

Some housing markets are so large that new infrastructure developments will have no measurable effect on housing prices or rents. The city of Newcastle has the largest coal loading facility in the world, and its current annual export capacity of about 100 metric tonnes is planned to double in coming years. Yet this expansion is unlikely to have any significant impact on Newcastle's housing market, because the city has a population of over 300 000, which is more than some capital cities, and its economic welfare is not dependent on coal exports. In fact, mining plays only a minor part in the port's activities and its long established mines have little impact on the housing market.

It's the same story in Townsville, the largest city in northern Queensland and the region's administrative, defence, commercial, business and retail centre with a population of nearly 180 000. The Townsville housing market does not rely on mining or port expansions because mineral exports only form a very minor part of its economic activities. In fact, some mining developments and other infrastructure projects can actually have a negative impact on local housing markets due to the high pollution and noise levels they create.

Because speculative housing investment is not based on current housing demand but on the expectation of increased housing demand in the future, investors must be prepared to wait for the anticipated renters or purchasers to materialise, or sell the property to another speculative investor. This sort of investment enables housing price bubbles to form and to burst if demand falls or if overdevelopment overtakes demand. The 'get in first and get out in time' notion is crucial, especially in areas where housing demand from a new mine or infrastructure development could be years away. Here are some simple rules to follow if you are confronted with a speculative housing investment opportunity.

Rules for deciding whether to speculate

First, do your research.

➤ Examine the type of infrastructure or development project that will happen in the area.

➤ Assess the location: the more remote, the better.

➤ Assess the housing market: the cheaper, the better.

➤ Assess the current rental market: the smaller, the better.

➤ Assess planned publicity: the bigger, the better.

➤ Estimate local and overseas investor appeal: the higher, the better.

➤ Determine the expected hold time for your purchase: the longer you can manage to hold, the better.

➤ Determine your hold costs and sell price target: the more they outweigh your initial cost, the better.

Once all of these points have been answered satisfactorily, you can make your purchase decision.

Construction

The construction stage provides the greatest opportunities for investors because of the high number of workers involved and the lack of suitable housing for them. These opportunities also carry the least risk, because potential housing surpluses resulting from completion of the project are years away.

Even so, infrastructure development projects in cities and large urban centres play a very different role in changing housing demand to those in regional or remote locations. In large population centres there's no rise in housing demand at all, because the workers engaged on the project commute from their existing homes in the city or town. In fact, reductions in housing demand can occur because the noise, dust, pollution, traffic congestion and delays go on for a number of years and drive many local residents, especially renters, away.

In regional areas there may not be enough skilled workers on hand to undertake the construction project, so they must be brought in and locally housed. Rental demand rises and causes rents and rental yields to increase as well, leading to higher investor interest. In theory, this in turn will result in housing price rises as investors compete with each other to buy properties. In practice, however, the accommodation solutions adopted by the construction companies and contractors can take a number of forms, with different effects on local housing markets.

They may compete with investors to purchase properties for their employees to live in, directly putting upward pressure on housing prices but none on rental demand. In other areas they take out long leases to guarantee accommodation for their employees, providing investors with high rent security but only for a limited selection of properties. They may also erect demountables to house drive-in drive-out or fly-in fly-out workers so that there is no change to local rental demand. If none of these strategies is adopted by the construction companies and if rental accommodation shortages become acute, workers pay for board or lodging with local families, book hotel rooms, motels, holiday cabins and even stay in caravan parks. Sorting out this confusing array of possibilities is not difficult, because you can easily research and track the progress of large publicly funded infrastructure projects on the National Infrastructure Construction Schedule at www.nics.gov.au. This site gives you a full description of the infrastructure project, the type of industry, its location, estimated total value, the current stage and the timeline from commencement to completion.

With the National Infrastructure Construction Schedule at your fingertips, the only question remaining is where the construction workers and their families will reside and whether this will cause a local housing shortage. Housing markets with the greatest boom potential from infrastructure development projects are those located near the site that are likely to end up with rental accommodation shortages, and those housing markets where fly-in fly-out and drive-in drive-out employees are likely to live with their families when not rostered on-duty.

Conducting some further online research about a project will show you where the impact on rental demand is likely to be the greatest. The good news is that rising rental demand coupled with growing investor demand are the ingredients for a housing market boom. The better news is that you can estimate where and when this is most likely to occur. While infrastructure development booms can occur anywhere, the best investment opportunities may also be located in areas set to benefit from other emerging booms such as retirees and tourism so that they offer both high growth potential and low risk.

When to sell

The aim is to hold your property until demand from other investors increases your expected selling price sufficiently to cover your purchase, holding and selling costs, plus your profit. If in the meantime the prospects for successful completion of the project have advanced, you can always hold the property for a further period of time, but your continued research into the nature and progress of the development or project is crucial.

Large projects, whether public or private, have a habit of being delayed, altered or even abandoned, usually with far less fanfare than when they were initially announced. For many investors, housing is about securing returns based on the demand for accommodation. They need to know where speculation ends and real demand starts.

The solution to this problem is simply to track the progress of new projects and remember that real demand only comes from the households that will move into the area. Wait until there's evidence of real demand, such as reducing rental vacancies and stock on the market. Whether you choose to speculate or wait, housing purchases based on real housing demand are secure, while the only demand that speculation creates is more speculation.

This key has shown you how find the areas with the greatest growth potential, and how to predict the likely direction of future price and rent changes in any suburb or town in Australia. The next key shows you:

➤ how different types of markets work

➤ when they are likely to provide the best returns

➤ how to find markets that perform well against the trend, even booming when there is no growth to be found elsewhere.

Key 3

Discover where and when to buy

The previous key showed you how to read any housing market and predict the likely direction of price and rent changes in any suburb or town. This key shows you:

➤ the different types of housing markets and how they work

➤ when they are likely to provide the best returns.

We look at owner-occupier-dominant and renter-dominant markets and show you how to find markets that are forecast to perform well and avoid those where price falls are likely.

The three dynamics of the housing market — people, purchasing power and properties — work together to cause price and rent changes and we can group households together by the way these factors combine. For example, first-home buyers are heavily reliant on the cost and availability of housing finance, while potential retirees have no need for finance at all and usually downgrade when they buy their final home. There are also times when high overseas immigration leads to a rise in rental demand in some locations, or when opportunity seekers move to a mining town or tourist resort and boost rental demand.

Understand different market dynamics

By understanding the dynamics of each of the different types of households, you will know when to invest in certain suburbs and when not to.

First-home buyer markets

The high cost of buying a home in Australia means that virtually every first-home buyer engages in a reluctant trade-off between that ideal home in a location they desire and the less satisfactory home in a location they can afford. Not only does this restrict first-home buyers to lower-priced houses in the outer suburbs and units along the major transport corridors of our cities, it also means that they will move to a better home in a more desirable location as soon as their circumstances permit.

Since 1991, first-home buyers have only made up about 15 per cent of property purchases annually, and they entered into just one-fifth of total housing finance commitments. Yet history shows that whenever their numbers rise significantly above those proportions, first-home buyers have acted as a growth catalyst, initiating price rises at the low end of the market that create equity for previous first-home buyers and precipitate movement upward all the way through the housing market.

Many new households will rent for years before they feel the need or are able to buy their first home, so their demand for housing flows largely into investment properties. The crucial demand dynamic in first-home buyer markets is the number of new or renting households that aspire to become homeowners. Our population growth from births has been slowly rising for many years, creating a steady increase in potential first-home buyers, but the rate of overseas migration has varied considerably. Many migrants arrive here in ready-made households and it takes them a few years to get settled to the point where they can successfully apply for a home loan. This means there is a time lag of three to four years before most overseas arrival households can hope to become first-home buyers.

Figure 3.1 shows the dramatic increase in the number of prospective first-home buyers that occurred in 2012 and 2013. This was mostly due to a rise in the number of overseas arrivals three to four years before.

Figure 3.1: prospective first-home buyers' origins

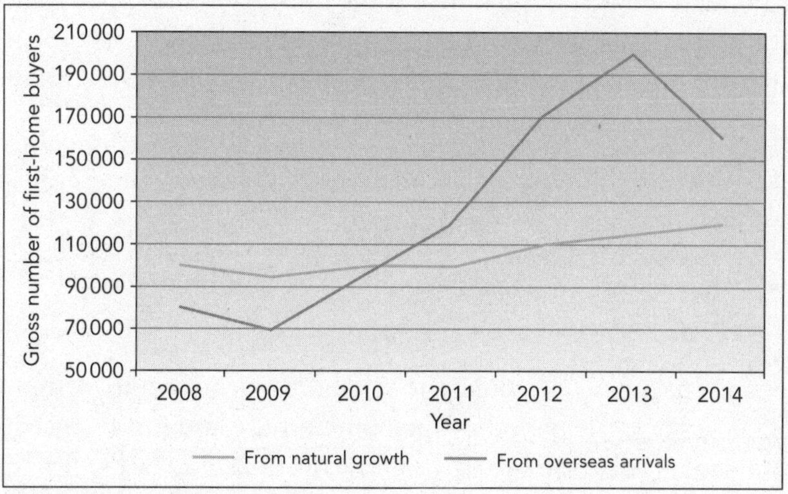

Source: Australian Bureau of Statistics.

Even though our population growth rate has now slowed to its long-term average of about 1.6 per cent per annum, when increases in overseas migration occur, they often lead to housing booms a few years later.

Although homeownership is an integral part of the great Australian dream it often seems to be out of the reach of first-time buyers. Lower-priced housing markets can experience little to no growth for years on end, and even occasionally suffer considerable price drops if buyers fall away. Whenever this happens, fingers are pointed at possible culprits such as:

➤ housing unaffordability

➤ high deposit requirements

➤ interest rates

➤ lack of government incentives

➤ economic slowdowns.

Although the cost of their first home must seem incredibly high for aspirational owners, they are not being asked to pay for it in cash. It is not the price of the property that deters them from purchase, but two components of the price:

➤ the monthly payment, which is related to the amount of finance that the lender is prepared to provide

➤ the deposit, which is the unfinanced portion of the purchase price.

Loan repayments are linked to the borrower's income, current interest rates, the period of the loan and the amount financed, but housing deposits are an artificial construct used by lenders to minimise risk and maximise return. They do this by setting the percentage of the property's value for which they are prepared to provide finance. When money is tight or lenders are nervous, they restrict finance by increasing the percentage of the price that borrowers have to find themselves. The effect of this tactic is shown in figure 3.2, where high deposit requirements in some years have acted like a barrier, putting many budding first-time buyers out of the race.

Figure 3.2: the first-home buyer deposit barrier

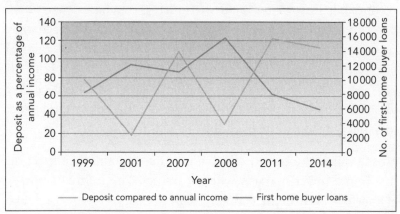

Source: Australian Bureau of Statistics; housing data provided by Australian Property Monitors.

Although the Reserve Bank might cut interest rates to historical lows, it requires more than the cost of finance to enable aspiring first-home buyers to enter the market; they must also be able to raise the deposit. Figure 3.2 shows why first-home buyers did not participate in the Sydney housing boom in 2014: the deposits required by lenders were such a disincentive. If the required deposit is more than 80 per cent of a household's annual income it becomes too difficult. The figure also shows that in 2001 and 2008 the amount of household income required as a deposit fell to 30 per cent or less and led to first home buyer booms in those years.

When finance is easy and lenders are full of confidence about the housing market, they will finance about 90 per cent of the purchase price, even for a first-home buyer. This was the catalyst for the booms in first-home buyer markets in 2001 and 2008, although there were other factors that contributed to those booms, such as low interest rates and increases to the First Home Owner Grant.

How does an increase in a group of homebuyers normally comprising just 15 per cent of housing purchases precipitate a boom in the housing market? It's because the rules change. Low interest rates, increased home buyer grants and relaxed minimum deposit requirements, when they occur, apply to all prospective first-home owners, and if it's easier for one, it's easier for all. In addition, people with similar demographics tend to act together — when some lead, the rest will follow.

This is called the cohort effect, and it has a dramatic impact on first-home buyer markets when it occurs. The influx of buyers at the low end of the market enables existing owners to take advantage of the increased prices and upgrade to a bigger home or a better location. The owners of the homes they in turn purchase also then upgrade, and because each successive wave of upgraders has access to larger amounts of equity, prices escalate upwards along with values. By the time this wave of price-growth has made its way to the top echelons of the housing market, it will have already deserted the first-home buyer suburbs where it all started, which means that timing is everything.

Figure 3.3 shows how the growth in numbers of first-home buyers in 2000 to 2002 and 2008 to 2009 was accompanied by rising median house prices generally. These increases were across the board, working their way upwards through the housing markets from lower median-valued localities to higher-priced ones.

Figure 3.3: first-home buyer–led housing booms

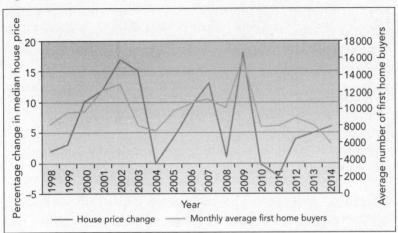

Source: Australian Bureau of Statistics; housing data provided by Australian Property Monitors.

If prospective first-home buyers' desire for ownership is matched with increased government incentives, a period of low or reduced interest rates and lower deposit requirements, then the number of first-time homeowners swells dramatically. The good news for investors is that the longer such a mix of buyer incentives is delayed, the greater the pent-up demand for first-home purchases and the bigger the housing market boom that follows.

Upgrader markets

First-home buyers are constrained by the cost and availability of finance, so their first home may not be their preferred type of dwelling, or in an ideal location. This means that, usually after an average of four years has passed, they tend to move to accommodate a growing family's space and schooling needs, or to be closer to work, or family and friends. They may make several moves as their housing needs change and their 'perfect location' changes with their lifestyle and aspirations. We call these homeowners *movers and improvers* or *upgraders*. They comprise all those households that have made the transition to their second or third home, but are still paying off their mortgage. They represent about four million households, which is well over one-third of all households in Australia. As time passes they become progressively more financially secure and less at the mercy of interest rates.

Both their repayments and the passive growth in the housing market increase the equity they have in their home. Instead of needing a deposit to buy another home, they use this equity in the home they sell as a deposit. In addition they have acquired a proven repayment record and their loan repayments are gradually reducing as a percentage of household income. For this group of homeowners, affordability now becomes a measure of the equity in their home compared with the price of a new home and their ability to meet the new loan repayments. It means that each move is usually upward to a more desirable home or a more sought-after location.

This continual turnover of properties presents excellent opportunities for investors, because owner-occupiers buy and sell properties for personal reasons. It may be a buyer's market rather than a good time to sell, but many homeowners would not be aware of this. The area they move to may be a seller's market, and, again, they may be unaware. This is why investors who research these facts will always achieve more than the long-term growth rate in any area, because they are buying and selling at the right time to make the maximum gain.

One of the main causes of the Sydney housing boom in 2013–14 was established owner-occupiers who took advantage of lower interest rates and their improved financial conditions to upgrade to a bigger house in a better location, with the bank lenders willing to provide finance to established homeowners.

We can predict when and where such upgrader-led booms will occur. The best time to buy in upgrader markets is when:

➤ There has been an extended period of little to no growth in the market.

➤ Economic conditions are stable and unemployment levels are low.

➤ Housing finance is freely available to existing homeowners.

The issue is that you don't buy an entire city; you buy a property in one suburb. If this information is to be of value you need to know which suburbs are likely to rise in price, when this is likely to occur and how long it is likely to last. Although the median price-growth in the Sydney market was about 17 per cent in 2013 and 11 per cent in 2014, these modest numbers disguised some huge variations in house prices, such as those shown in table 3.1.

Table 3.1: Sydney's best and worst performers 2012 to 2014

Year	Best performer	Price rise in year	Worst performer	Price fall in year	Difference in performance
2012	Cabarita	30%	Edgecliff	−27%	57%
2013	Rhodes	40%	Abbotsford	−10%	50%
2014	Edgecliff	45%	Tamarama	−7%	52%

Source: Housing data provided by Australian Property Monitors and Property Power Database, Property Power Partners.

The difference between the best and worst performing suburb in each year was quite staggering — it was 50 per cent or more! While some suburbs started rising in price during 2012, most were still falling in value; but even during 2014, when most suburbs were rising in price, some were falling. Most suburbs only rose in price in one or two of the three years, and many only went up in one year, to fall in value the next. There were some suburbs where house prices rose in every year from 2012 to 2014, but not very many, and some suburbs hardly went up in price at all.

If you jumped into the Sydney market in 2013 you may have done very well, or you may have achieved very little overall growth. How would you have any idea of which suburbs were most likely to rise in price and which to avoid?

Key 2 shows how to read the house or unit market in any suburb by the relationship of listings to sales. There are five types of markets: stressed and buyer markets have a surplus of properties for sale, neutral markets are in balance, and seller and boom markets have a shortage of properties for sale. Table 3.2 shows how to read suburb house or unit markets quite quickly by seeing whether there is a surplus or shortage of stock, and whether prices are likely to be rising or falling as a result.

Table 3.2: how to read housing markets

More current listings than annual sales	About the same	More annual sales than current listings
Stock surplus prices falling	Balanced stock no change to prices	Stock shortage prices rising

Source: Property Power Database, Property Power Partners.

Had you done this exercise in 2012, it would have helped to identify those Sydney upgrader suburbs that were about to boom and which ones to leave alone, as table 3.3 indicates.

Table 3.3: reading the Sydney upgrader housing market 2012 to 2014

Year	Best performer	Market reading	Worst performer	Market reading
2012	Cabarita	Stock shortage	Edgecliff	Stock surplus
2013	Rhodes	Stock shortage	Abbotsford	Stock surplus
2014	Edgecliff	Stock shortage	Tamarama	Stock surplus

Source: Property Power Database, Property Power Partners.

House prices in Cabarita rose by over 30 per cent in 2012 because there was a huge stock shortage, while they fell by nearly the same amount in Edgecliff, where there was a high surplus of stock. By 2014 the situation had reversed itself, and Edgecliff now had an acute stock shortage that caused prices to rise by 45 per cent in one year. Such high price-growth is sweet but it doesn't last long, once again demonstrating the importance of timing the market.

You now have some simple, logical techniques to use when it appears that upgraders may be on the move and prices may change as a result.

Retiree markets

Some housing markets have provided excellent returns when growth was hard to find elsewhere. Seaside resorts such as Byron Bay, Coffs Harbour, the Gold Coast and Sunshine Coast enjoyed spectacular periods of growth in the recent past, but the data also tells us that growth in these markets inexplicably stopped even though the rest of the market was booming. The reason for their growth was their popularity as retirement destinations and the cause of their decline was when they stopped being attractive to retirees. Potential retirees make up one-fifth of the housing market; their houses are mostly owned without debt, they are located in many of the higher priced localities of our major cities, and the number of people approaching retirement age as a proportion of our population is actually increasing.

Australians have always looked to retirement with hopes for security, health, independence and sufficient fitness and finances to enjoy their extra free time. The prospect of selling the family home with its comforts and memories is another matter, often dreaded and put off as long as possible. Eventually, a number of factors can force their hand:

➤ health and money issues

➤ maintenance of a larger-than-necessary home

➤ the changing nature of the local area.

When they decide to seek a new location they'll search out areas that offer:

➤ better lifestyle

➤ appropriate health, recreation and entertainment facilities

➤ demographically similar neighbours.

This last factor is the most important, and explains the extremely high growth in retiree housing markets that have occurred in the past — retirees tend to move to the same locations at the same time, creating some spectacular housing price booms.

The growth can only occur when the numbers of retirees over a short period of time are enough to make a difference. These housing markets are unique because retirees, unlike first- or second-home buyers, are not fussed if banks are tight on finance, or if interest rates are rising as they have no need for finance. They are not concerned if unemployment is rising, or economic conditions are deteriorating, as they are leaving the workforce for good. Even so, each retirement location has its limits, because virtually all retirees endeavour to have cash left over from the sale of their home to spend or keep for the future. If there's been too much price-growth in their desired location, new retirees will seek another more affordable area, creating more demand for housing as they move. That's certainly not been the case until recently, so what has caused the change?

The answer is to be found in a series of economic downturns that have occurred and are still playing out across the world. The Global Financial Crisis of 2008 severely depleted the value of all investors' shares and superannuation holdings, and had the effect of encouraging potential retirees to wait until their investments recovered, or at least improved. This created a backlog of potential retirees, as shown in figure 3.4, who are now biting the bullet and starting to retire.

Figure 3.4: Australian retirement trends

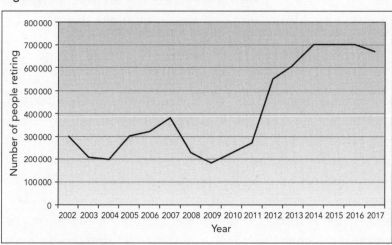

Source: Australian Bureau of Statistics.

Retirement housing markets around Australia will boom no matter how the rest of the market performs, but where will these booms occur? The recurring pattern of growth and decline in retirement locations, especially if retirees form a significant proportion of the total population, provides the answer. The pattern starts when a new retirement area is 'discovered' by generational trendsetters, making it better known and desirable. As retirees settle in the area, it becomes more popularised and the housing market starts to boom. Rather than deterring more retirees, rising prices and publicity encourages them to join in and the influx grows. Demand increases further as local business and commerce changes to accommodate the needs of retirees with specialised health care, therapeutic, education, entertainment and recreation services. The initial retirees also help to transform the town, having both time and money on their hands. These are now the locations that it seems everyone wants to retire to. Housing demand in such locations keeps rising along with prices until the cost of purchase exceeds the capacity of new retirees to buy, giving them the incentive to discover cheaper locations elsewhere.

After the growth period runs its course the housing market in these now established and well-known locations stagnates. The need for respite care and nursing homes grows as the population ages. New retirees will shun such locations, not just because prices are still relatively high, but because there are so many people older than they are, serving an unwelcome reminder of what lies in store down the line. This pattern repeats every fifteen years or so, reaching its low point when retirees move to hospices and then pass away. As the median age of the community and the proportion of older people falls, increasing numbers of properties come onto the market, placed there by relatives and heirs of the original retirees. There are often so many on the market at the same time that prices start to fall, but they will not be attractive to a new wave of retirees until the old retiree tide has totally receded and the pattern starts all over again.

When any retirement location's prices start to approach those of the areas from which retirees are relocating, demand flows into nearby areas that still have lower prices. Again, as these prices rise, demand increases in other areas until prices rise there as well. This causes retirement housing markets to boom at different times and has left them with varying numbers of older people. The retirement boom in far north NSW started in Byron Bay and Lennox Head, and then moved out to Ballina, Brunswick Heads and finally Tweed Heads as prices escalated.

As the opportunity to find previously undiscovered locations around coastal Australia has long gone, the next wave of retirees will seek areas that are already developed, and meet their requirements for:

➤ location

➤ services

➤ facilities

➤ prices

➤ generational attraction.

Potential locations are not hard to find, and there are hundreds of them near our major capital cities and beyond. First select areas that have good access to capital cities by road, or have local airports. Then remove those that do not have excellent health care services such as a local hospital and keep those that have educational, recreational and entertainment facilities aimed at mature residents. In table 3.4 (overleaf) I have done this for towns on the New South Wales south coast, and this indicates that both Moruya and Merimbula meet the criteria.

Table 3.4: location and facilities

Location	Transport	Services	Facilities
Jervis Bay	Highway	Good	Excellent
Swanhaven	Highway	Good	Good
Batemans Bay	Highway	Excellent	Excellent
Moruya	Airport	Excellent	Excellent
Tuross Head	Highway	Good	Good
Narooma	Highway	Good	Good
Bermagui	Highway	Excellent	Good
Tathra	Highway	Good	Good
Merimbula	Airport	Excellent	Excellent
Pambula	Highway	Excellent	Good

To ensure that there is sufficient capacity for price-growth, also restrict your search to those towns and localities with median housing prices below the median prices of the nearest capital city. Then to find areas with the highest generational attraction, select only those communities that have low proportions of people aged 65 and over, but where this is rising.

You can do this simple research at home, using Australian Bureau of Statistics–provided population age profiles for any suburb, town or urban area in Australia. Simply Google 'Basic Community Profile' and update the data to the present time, remembering that the proportion of older people in retirement towns has been reducing over recent years. Median prices can be obtained from the Databank at the back of your *Australian Property Investor* magazine. These simple research steps will enable you to produce your own list of potential retirement areas. When you've identified that a new wave of retirees is about to move into a certain area, you'll be ready to catch the housing market boom they create.

Renters and their effect on housing markets

Rent is the bread and butter of investors, providing a regular and usually reliable return. Best of all are those areas that provide a positive cash flow, where the income from rent exceeds all expenses including interest repayments, and the property is paying itself off. We can actively raise our rent returns through cosmetic improvements, renovations, adding a granny flat or engaging in student stacking, but finding genuine passive cash cow locations is often difficult. Rental guarantees and high rental yields caused by falling prices can make research complicated.

About 2 500 000 households in Australia are private renters, which means that their dwellings are owned by investors. It is a mistake to think of renters as just a source of rent, because they can have an indirect but significant effect on property prices. For example, in a town with a large and volatile rental population (such as a tourist resort or mining town) the following sequence of events can occur if rental demand rises:

➤ As more renters are attracted to the area, rental vacancy rates reduce.

➤ Asking rents rise as tenants compete to rent properties, and rental yields rise.

➤ Prices rise as investors compete to buy properties.

➤ Investors increase the rental supply by buying properties to rent out.

➤ Developers are attracted to the area and create more rental supply.

➤ Rental surpluses translate into longer vacancy periods.

➤ Investors compete for tenants and asking rents start to fall.

➤ Investors start selling their properties.

➤ Surplus stock on the market leads to longer time on the market.

➤ Investors compete for buyers and asking prices start to fall.

➤ More investors decide to sell out.

➤ Investors selling out reduces the rental supply.

Eventually, the balance of rental demand and supply is restored as the properties sold by investors are bought by owner-occupiers and the rental supply reduces. This can take years, especially in areas that have been overdeveloped, and it means that you need to be aware of:

➤ the types of renters that live in the area where you are investing

➤ whether their numbers are rising or falling

➤ whether there is a current and potential shortage or surplus of suitable rental properties.

Rent returns can vary widely due to the different types and locations of investment properties, and to the types of households that rent in an area and the reasons that they rent there.

Rental demand can change property values

Even the experts can misjudge rental demand, with disastrous consequences for investors who follow their predictions. A few years ago, locations such as Gladstone and Moranbah were being touted as Australia's hottest investment locations with claimed rental yields of over 20 per cent. The rising rental demand in these towns was usually attributed to high population growth and property shortages due to new resource projects providing more jobs. Something went horribly wrong in many of those areas, with prices and rents failing to rise and even falling dramatically in some of them. Why were the optimistic rental market predictions for these areas and many like them so completely incorrect? And why did the drops in rent lead to collapsing house prices? To find out, we need to look at the dynamics behind housing markets where renters call the tune.

Unlike owner-occupiers who want the security and stability that home ownership provides, or investors whose aim is profit, renters are often after a particular lifestyle. The benefit of living in a particular dwelling or area is related more to proximity to work, recreation, friends and entertainment and has little to do with the property apart from its facilities, views and the weekly rent.

Most renters can be categorised in one of these four main groups.

The permanent renters—low risk, low price investment areas

The lower socio-economic localities of Australia are home to large proportions of permanent renters, households that will never buy a property, with many also relying on some form of temporary or permanent government assistance. These households reside in ex–housing commission suburbs located on the outskirts of suburbia, in ex–holiday homes along coastal fringes and in rural towns that have affordable rentals. Many of these households are long-term residents unwilling or unable to relocate. Because of government rental assistance, rental yields in these markets tend to be higher than in urban rental markets. Vacancy rates are very low, and defaults are rare. Typical house prices will vary from $200 000 to $400 000 providing rental yields of about 6 or 7 per cent. These are the typical cash cow suburbs, generating a reliable and secure source of income to investors.

New households—high rental yields, but risk of overdevelopment

Although the assumed key to Gen Y renter markets is natural growth, this is misleading, because their numbers in the large eastern capital cities are boosted by the large and continual interstate movement of younger people from the smaller states and the territories, and also by well-educated younger overseas arrivals who prefer urban living. The demand for inner suburban modern units in Sydney, Melbourne and Brisbane near recreational and entertainment facilities is therefore higher than the numbers might suggest, and it is growing. Many live in rent sharing groups and so investors are looking at purchase prices from $500 000 upwards, with rents that are forecast to rise rapidly in the medium term.

The unwillingness of younger people to buy properties increasingly turns to inability, as high rents make deposit-saving difficult and as banks remain reluctant to lend to first-home buyers. This increasing pressure on the demand for such rental accommodation offers investors excellent long-term rent opportunities that are relatively low risk in the current economic environment.

Overseas arrival destinations—moderate risk, high yield

The middle distance, older, well-established suburbs of our major cities have always been an initial destination for overseas arrivals. They look for ethnically friendly localities, close to shops, schools, places of worship, public transport and employment. In such suburbs, they can form most of the households and because their mobility is limited, they periodically send rents shooting upwards, generating rental yields of over 8 per cent, and form excellent cash cow opportunities in the process. Extremely reliable renters, their aim is to save enough money to buy a dwelling as soon as possible, often within four years and usually elsewhere. The number of overseas arrivals and their ethnic origins are important to investors because if the number of overseas arrivals who prefer a particular area starts to drop, then rental demand will slow. The key to this market is to watch the trend in number and country of origin of overseas migrants and their propensity to rent in ethnically friendly areas.

Opportunity seekers—creating both rent and price rise potential

This last group of renters is comparatively small in size and they live mainly in regional and rural areas. They are workers who seek high incomes on infrastructure development projects or mine and port expansions. They are students residing away from home in university towns and they are also workers in tourist resorts who combine good incomes with recreational lifestyles in attractive locations. Because they rent in small and sometimes remote locations, they can have a huge effect on asking rents when their numbers rise dramatically. It was the demand for housing by mine workers that created high rents and yields during the last mining boom and resulted in the surge of investor buying activity in the mining towns and ports shown in figure 3.5 (overleaf).

Figure 3.5: peak levels of investor ownership during the mining boom

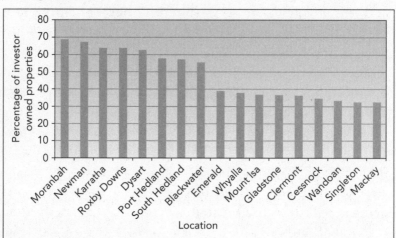

Source: Australian Bureau of Statistics.

The percentage of investor-owned properties in towns such as Moranbah reached their highest levels in 2013 just as the demand for rental properties was easing due to coalmining cutbacks and closures. This picture was repeated all over mining towns and ports around Australia and in some cases resulted in surplus rental stocks, which led to increased vacancies with falling rents.

Many investors tried to bail out by placing their vacant properties on the market, which only led to falling prices as investors competed with each other to find buyers.

Renters on the move

Because renters tend to move more often than owner-occupiers, they can have a significant effect on rents in suburbs and towns where their numbers are high; if enough of them decide to move in or out, this leads to rental shortages or surpluses. If sufficient renters move away, the fall in rental demand can lead to panicked investor sales (as it did in many of the towns shown in figure 3.5) and then prices fall as well. This normally only happens if a significant proportion of properties in the town or suburb are investor-owned and large numbers of renters leave, but it can also occur in a town where the number of investor-owned properties rises, either because existing properties are being snapped up by uninformed investors, or because new housing developments are being marketed to investors. Either way, when the rental supply starts to exceed the rental demand, rents begin to fall and the problems for investors start.

Growth can only occur in country or regional housing markets when the number of buyers increases beyond the supply of properties on the market and competition between prospective purchasers pushes up prices. This usually occurs in captive rental markets where workers on a new mine, railway, port or resort development are forced to rent locally because there are no large cities in the vicinity. As the supply of available rental properties is exhausted, rents start to rise and the rental yield goes up as well. Investors start to take notice and buy properties, causing price rises as demand grows. This then encourages more investors to buy and the process continues as long as the rental demand remains greater than the supply of rentable properties.

The bubble bursts if the supply of rental properties starts to exceed the demand for them. This can be due to a combination of circumstances. Every investor-purchased property becomes a rental property, so over-investment can lead to a surplus of rental properties, as can overdevelopment by exuberant developers. The first indicator of the start of this cycle is when the number of rental vacancies suddenly falls, as this usually means that the first wave of surveyors, inspectors and engineers has arrived. By keeping track of rental vacancies in communities where such projects are proposed you can then confirm the cause with a phone call to a local property manager and be one of the first investors to reap the benefits of the anticipated growth in both rents and prices. Figure 3.6 shows how the number of rental vacancies in the southern NSW town of Hay declined from December 2013 to August 2014.

Figure 3.6: the fall in rental vacancies in Hay, NSW

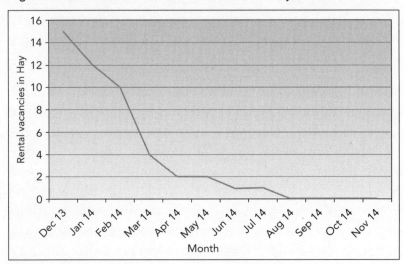

Source: Property Power Database, Property Power Partners.

The reason for this decline in rental vacancies was that Auscott was planning to build a huge cotton gin in Hay in time for the 2015 cotton crop, and construction was due to commence in February 2014. Construction workers engaged on the project quickly leased all available properties in town and were then put on rental waiting lists. Table 3.5 shows the effect this had on the local housing market in Hay as asking rents started to rise from January 2014, causing the rental yield to rise to 8 per cent a few months later.

Table 3.5: rent, yield and price movements in Hay, NSW

Month	Median weekly asking rent	Rental yield	Median house price
Dec 2013	$100	6%	$90 000
Jan 2014	$125	7%	$90 000
Feb 2014	$135	8%	$90 000
Mar 2014	$145	8%	$95 000
Apr 2014	$145	7%	$110 000
May 2014	$150	7%	$120 000
Jun 2014	$155	6%	$140 000
Jul 2014	$160	5%	$170 000
Aug 2014	$160	5%	$175 000
Sep 2014	$170	5%	$180 000
Oct 2014	$180	5%	$180 000
Nov 2014	$185	5%	$190 000

Source: Property Power Database, Property Power Partners.

The rise in rental yield attracted investors who started buying investment properties from March onwards and by November 2014 the median house price had doubled, while rents had grown by over 20 per cent. Table 3.5 also shows that because prices rose faster than rents the rental yield started falling, yet few housing markets anywhere in Australia were providing investors such incredible outcomes over such a short period. Of course, when the cotton gin is completed, rental demand will return to longer-term levels and rents will fall. Because of the potential for overinvestment in Hay, prices will probably fall as well, but the number of rental vacancies holds the key and astute investors in Hay will be watching the rental vacancy trend closely. Tracking rental vacancies enables investors to find investment opportunities in towns such as Hay just before price-growth starts and sell before it ends, but for those of us who don't like interpreting numbers and trends there's a far easier way to benefit from growth in regional housing markets.

Measure rental supply and demand

How do you accurately measure changes in rental demand and supply? While property buying and selling involves titles, contracts and settlement periods and is controlled by government agencies providing accurate sales data, renting is very much a private affair with little data available apart from weekly asking rents, rental vacancies and vacancy rates. Most rental-market predictions are based on population growth figures but the census is the only accurate measure made of where people are living and renting, and it's only conducted every five years. The first safety measure investors should use in measuring rental demand is not to rely on predictive reports that use outdated information.

The second is not to rely on hearsay. Just because a new mine is about to open or expand, or a new freeway, hospital or university is planned, such new infrastructure can only have a speculative impact on housing markets until the project is underway. In any case, rental demand is only likely to grow during the construction phase of such projects and may disappear when the work is complete. Lastly, don't fall into the trap of relying on the past performance of renters in an effort to predict their future behaviour. This is because the conditions that changed rental demand in the past are very likely to be different in future and, even when the demand for rental accommodation in a city, region or suburb is identical to some previous point in time, the supply of rental stock may be different.

Luckily, there is a very simple way you can track rental demand in any suburb or town and get a good idea of whether demand is rising or falling and, even more importantly, whether there is a surplus or shortage of rental stock. This is because there is a strong relationship between the number of investor-owned properties in a town and the number of renters. By estimating the number of investor-owned properties and then looking up an online listing site to obtain the number of rental vacancies, you can quickly determine the percentage of investor-owned properties that are vacant. Figure 3.7 shows you the percentage of vacant investor-owned properties in the same towns that had a high percentage of investor-owned properties in figure 3.5 (see p. 84). The towns are ranked from left to right by the percentage of rental vacancies.

Figure 3.7: rental vacancies are an early warning system

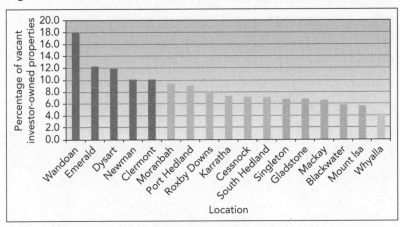

Source: QuickStats 2006, 2011, Australian Bureau of Statistics.

The towns on the left are suffering from rental vacancies amounting to over 10 per cent of all investor-owned properties, which means severe stress for the owners, with high vacancy rates and rents falling dramatically. As we move to the right along the scale the situations improve, with the percentage of vacant investor-owned properties falling. Whyalla is the only town with a rental vacancy rate below 5 per cent, which still equates to a fortnight's turnaround between rentals. All of the towns on the left suffered dramatic drops in weekly asking rents since 2013, which then led to falling prices as investors tried to sell their empty properties.

You can estimate this relationship between renters and investors in any area by looking up the total number of rental vacancies provided by major listing sites for a suburb, town or city, and then determining the total number of investor-owned properties in the same area using QuickStats. Although this is census data, the number of investor-owned properties usually doesn't change as much as the number of vacancies, and it is the ratio of vacancies to total investor-owned properties that tells you the current state of the rental market and whether rents are likely to fall or rise as a result. You can also use this simple technique to find areas with possible rental shortages, or those where you suspect that rental demand may rise, such as new or expanding mining towns, ports, tourist centres or regional growth centres. Table 3.6 shows an example of how rental vacancies levels can be used to forecast asking rents.

Table 3.6: example of how rental vacancies forecast asking rents

Suburb name	Hay, NSW	
Month	Current rental vacancies	Median asking weekly rent
1	15	$150
2	14	$150
3	8	$150
4	5	$160
5	2	$180
6	0	$200
7	(Wait list)	$220
8	(Wait list)	$270

Source: Property Power Database, Property Power Partners.

In the western NSW town of Hay, the number of rental vacancies dropped as construction of the new cotton gin commenced and there was soon a wait list for prospective tenants, with asking rents rising by 80 per cent in just eight months. The secret to rent changes in such locations is the number of rental vacancies, which works as both an early warning system of areas to avoid and an early opportunity system for areas with possible investment potential.

High rental yields are not necessarily a good growth indicator

Despite the general consistency of rental demand in regional markets, it is always important to check the cause of high rental yields. Rental yield is a function of both prices and rents: it is the rent obtained in a year expressed as a percentage of the median sale price. The rental yield allows you to compare different possible investment locations by their cash-flow potential. The issue is that if median house prices fall and rents don't, or if they fall more than rents, then the rent yield actually rises. There are hundreds of small towns scattered around Australia with very high rental yields caused by savage house price falls over recent years. A small amount of research reveals areas where locals have been steadily moving out of towns due to mine closures, farm consolidations, drought or declining tourism, leaving a legacy of shuttered shops and empty houses with fading 'for lease' and 'for sale' signs. Apart from such 'no go' areas, it seems that there is a trade-off in regional housing investment which offers higher cash flow in return for lower capital growth, but we can have our cake and eat it too if we time an investment purchase when price-growth is about to start and sell when it is about to end.

The ripple effect

One of the best-known causes of house price-growth is known as the *ripple effect*. The theory is that rising housing prices spread steadily outwards, like ripples in a pond, from inner suburbs to those further from the city centre and from larger regional towns to smaller ones. The price ripples are caused by home buyers who are forced outwards in their search for affordable dwellings, and by investors who are attracted to the same areas by rising prices. Together they cause further price rises as they compete to buy properties and so the ripple moves slowly outwards.

Figure 3.8 demonstrates how the ripple effect occurred in Queanbeyan, a large city in New South Wales located on the ACT border.

Figure 3.8: how the ripple effect works

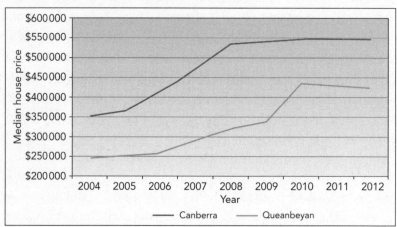

Source: Property Power Database, Property Power Partners.

Canberra's growth has led to Queanbeyan becoming an integral part of the national capital, with many of its 40 000 residents commuting to work there. In 2004, the median house price in Queanbeyan was only 70 per cent of that in the ACT, and the graph shows that rapidly rising house prices in Canberra from 2006 to 2009 led to similar price rises in Queanbeyan a year later as home buyer demand rippled out of Canberra. Depending on the amount of demand and the housing markets where it occurs, the price ripple may take several years to run its course.

This lag effect means that prices may still be rising in outlying regional areas after growth has ceased in the nearby capital city, which can lead to very short-lived growth in the outer areas. If interest rates rise at the same time or housing finance is otherwise restricted, prices can fall as overextended first-home buyers are forced to sell and investors lose heart and pull out as well. Figure 3.8 shows that there was only one year of high price-growth in Queanbeyan (2009–10) and that since then house prices have fallen slightly. This shows us that timing is everything.

This key showed you the very different types of buyer and renter markets — the types of households they comprise and what causes their prices and rents to change — so you will know which ones are likely to provide the best results and which to avoid. The next key shows you how to narrow down your search and identify the locality and type of property with the greatest potential to deliver the results you want.

Key 4

Narrow down your search

Once you have selected a suburb with good growth potential as shown in the previous keys, you need to narrow down your search. This key shows you how to identify the locality and type of property with the greatest potential to deliver the results you want, no matter what the market conditions are. You will discover how to:

➤ identify the types of areas preferred by local households

➤ use the splash effect to narrow down your search

➤ flip and trade for profit during booms

➤ hunt for bargains in stressed and buyer markets

➤ find the next boom market

➤ conduct your own effective on-the-ground research.

Even when you have selected a suburb that meets your investment aims you will need to refine your search within the suburb, because certain precincts or localities will be different from others. Some streets will be located closer to desirable features, such as:

➤ shops

➤ schools

➤ recreation

➤ transport

and others closer to less desirable ones, such as:

➤ industrial areas

➤ unwanted shops

➤ traffic noise and issues

➤ flight paths

➤ late-night hotels.

Even in the same street, some dwellings will have views while others will be without and one side will have a much better aspect than the other. There will also be distinct pockets of current or former housing commission homes, ex–holiday homes, aged care facilities and other types of accommodation that may or may not be desirable. The prevalence of public housing, for example, may not be unwanted if your target market is permanent rental demand or the opportunity to renovate.

It may also be an area undergoing gentrification, in which case you will notice some refurbished or even totally replaced homes among the others. While the perceived desirability of a property is to some extent factored into its price, its personal desirability for you depends on your investment goals and whether it is the type of housing in the area that suits your aims and whether you can make the property more attractive for future occupants.

Buying the wrong type of property in the right area will impact your chances of success just like buying the right property in the wrong area—you need to get both correct. Table 4.1 shows the critical differences that occupiers look for when choosing their new homes.

Table 4.1: preferred locations and dwellings for different households

Households	Preferred location	Preferred dwelling
Young families	Low traffic, parks and play areas	Safe
Professional couples	Local dining and entertainment	Easy to maintain
Retirees	Near shops and facilities	Accessible and attractive
Students	Close to transport	Quiet and functional

You can narrow your search down further by talking to property managers about which households are most likely to rent in the area and by talking to real estate agents to discuss which are most likely to purchase. Having decided which household market to target, you can choose the best location in the area and then select a property that provides the greatest potential uplift in appeal and value with an appropriate cosmetic renovation.

Give your new occupants a sense of belonging

The key here is that whatever you do should be immediately visible and obvious because cosmetic improvements are calling out 'look at me!' You may undertake needed improvements such as painting, planting and pruning, but remember that cosmetics are about providing confidence. By providing something that other vendors or landlords would not consider you can make a huge difference. A house for young families can be made safer with child-proof locks on gates, while planter boxes with ready-to-pick herbs will please retirees. A comprehensive selection of local restaurant menus placed in the kitchen immediately appeals to busy couples.

Giving the new occupants a sense of belonging instantly increases the appeal of your property, may not cost much, yet can be really effective in a flat or sluggish market. In addition to using such a strategy, you should always be on the lookout for areas where growth is most likely to occur, so that you can ride the price-growth wave created by both your own improvements and by those that the market itself is generating through higher buyer demand.

Look for areas where imminent price-growth is most likely to occur

The history of the Australian housing market, as explained in Key 1, shows that there have been extended periods of time with little to no house price-growth, and even occasional periods when prices have gone backwards. Although the housing market experienced housing price-growth following such years, it has by no means been equally shared across our cities and towns and there are locations in Australia that have experienced no real price-growth for over a decade.

Such a long-term lack of growth does not mean that rises are imminent, or even that they must eventually occur, but rather the opposite: that we can't be sure housing market increases will always occur. This is because housing prices only go up when the demand for housing rises and leads to shortages of stock on the market. This demand can come from:

➤ first-home buyers

➤ upgraders

➤ retirees.

Each surge in demand may take place at different times and in different locations. Nevertheless, we do know what causes such spikes in demand and therefore we can estimate where and when they will most likely take place after the housing market next takes a breather. Table 4.2 shows how the next housing boom is likely to unfold after many years of housing market stagnation, and which areas are likely to boom first.

Table 4.2: the key growth dynamics of different types of households

Type of buyer	Key growth dynamics	Boom areas
First-home buyers	Low deposits, easy finance, low repayments	Outer suburbs
Upgraders	Growth in equity and income, change of circumstances	Middle and inner suburbs
Retirees	High growth in equity, high residual net worth	Coastal resorts

This analysis is based on the performance of the housing market in the past, following many years of little to no growth, and what took place during the ensuing boom years, such as the 1950s, 1970s and 2000s. In each case, it was first-home buyers who led the market charge in outer suburbs and started a wave of price-growth that rippled through entire city housing markets.

In 2010 the Rudd government induced a first-home buyer boom, by tripling the first-home owner grant and guaranteeing bank deposits. The guarantee meant that banks were free to lend to first-home buyers because their activities were backed by the government. Since then, there hasn't been much joy in the market for first-home buyers. Their best hope is that once the current growth wave subsides their time may arrive. After a long period of stagnation first-home buyer areas are likely to provide the greatest growth potential for investors.

Housing price-growth and high deposit requirements tend to marginalise aspiring first-home buyers, but they have a vote and eventually the sheer weight of their growing numbers will force governments to act. Federal governments can introduce or increase first-home buyer grants and encourage housing finance providers to lower their deposit level requirements. State governments can reduce, refund or remove stamp duty for first-home buyers and provide their own grants as well.

When you see that governments are introducing such incentives aimed at first-home buyers, the suburbs to look for imminent price-growth are first-home buyer markets and those first-home buyer pockets within higher priced suburbs. The logic of this strategy is simple, but highly effective, because incentives that make it easier for aspiring first-home buyers to enter the market increase the demand but have no immediate effect on the supply, resulting in price rises as potential buyers compete with each other. Even if house prices rise by an amount equal to or even more than the total value of the incentives and grants, it does not deter more first home buyers. You can see how this plays out in the example shown in table 4.3.

Table 4.3: the effect of rising house prices on deposits

First-home buyer market	Purchase price	10% deposit	Grants and incentives	Total rise in house price	Rise in deposit needed
Start of boom	$400 000	$40 000	$30 000	–	–
Middle of boom	$440 000	$44 000	$30 000	$40 000	$4000
End of boom	$480 000	$48 000	$30 000	$80 000	$8000

The only other factor that can impact first-home buyer market demand in such a scenario is that repayments tend to rise as the amount borrowed per first-home buyer increases, even though it is still the same percentage of the purchase price in each case. This is usually when lenders come to the rescue with innovative packages such as amortised repayments, allowing for gradually increasing repayments over time. Sometimes lenders may even introduce negative amortisation loans, which simply means that the initial repayments don't cover the interest and extends the period of the loan. As long as housing prices in these areas are forecast to keep rising, the lenders are not at risk. Getting in on the ground floor as an investor at such times gives you the opportunity to participate in the first wave of price-growth in housing markets that have seen no price-growth for many years.

Use the splash effect to help narrow down your search

In Key 3, the ripple effect — the process of price-growth spreading outwards from a growth epicentre to other similar nearby suburbs, or from a major city to regional centres that have not yet gone up in price at all, or not to the same extent—is explained. It is commonly seen as an inevitable consequence of housing price-growth. You can use a very similar phenomenon that I call the *splash effect* to pick areas in nearby suburbs with similar types of housing to those where prices are shooting upwards, but where prices haven't yet started to rise. The difference between the ripple effect and the splash effect is that the growth in a price splash is limited to those types of housing for which demand is rising, so that the suburb as whole may not rise in price at all. Figure 4.1 shows how the splash effect worked in similar localities of Sydney's inner west suburbs during the housing price boom from 2012 to 2014.

Figure 4.1: how the splash effect works

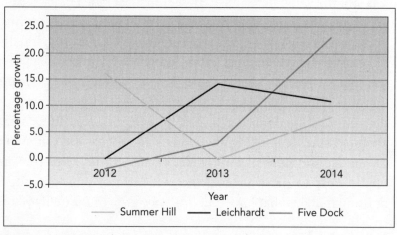

Source: Property Power Database, Property Power Partners.

The price of three-bedroom houses in Summer Hill boomed in 2012 even though there was little overall price-growth in the inner west at that time. The rise in price drove buyers for such houses to nearby suburbs such as Leichhardt and Five Dock, and the resultant shortage created a similar three-bedroom house boom in Leichhardt during 2013 — but not in Five Dock, where there was still sufficient stock of such properties on the market to meet the rising demand.

This left Five Dock as the only suburb with no real price-growth in three-bedroom houses in the entire inner west up to that point. According to the splash effect logic, three-bedroom houses in Five Dock would shoot up in price once the market turned from neutral to seller. This did indeed occur and pushed Five Dock's median house price during 2014 up more than the other inner west suburbs. The danger in applying splash effect logic indiscriminately is that nearby suburbs may not have stock shortages and may actually have surpluses, so that, although sales rise, there is no consequent price-growth. Nevertheless, there may be pockets in nearby suburbs or towns that have similar demographics to those where price rises are occurring and where a price splash may take place.

Once you are satisfied that the suburb or the locality within the suburb where you are purchasing meets the requirements for demographics and housing type and, house prices haven't risen yet, you need to check that the ratio of sales and listings shown in Key 2 indicate that this is a neutral market and about to go seller. The splash effect can be very useful as long as you remember that it is specific and not inevitable.

When growth is occurring more or less everywhere and in every type of market, a different strategy is called for to help narrow down your search.

Flip and trade properties for profit in booming markets

Flipping (selling a property almost immediately) and trading (holding a property for less than a year) have little to do with property investment, but while they fail at the wrong time they will certainly work at the right time, which is when:

➤ housing markets are booming

➤ bidders are crowding auctions

➤ properties are sold as soon as they come onto the market.

The practice is simply to buy and hold only for enough time to gain passive price-growth, then sell and repeat the process. Table 4.4 shows how an investor could flip four units in one year, and achieve a gross profit before tax of over $50000 (allowing for buy and sell costs of 7 per cent of each purchase price).

Table 4.4: flipping for profit during housing market booms

Unit	Buy	Growth	Costs (7%)	Profit
1	$300000	$330000	$21000	$9000
2	$330000	$370000	$23100	$16900
3	$370000	$410000	$25900	$14100
4	$410000	$450000	$28700	$11300

Choose the right development

Narrowing down your search in such markets and at such times is more about selecting the right development, because you can buy off the plan years before the project is complete, or even fully underway, with just a small deposit bond. This bond requires you to pay the full deposit by a certain agreed date, and then to pay the entire remaining purchase price at settlement, which could be years away. You can flip the property at any time once you have paid the deposit bond, as you are the legal purchaser. Many developers will sell off the initial units or lots at a discount to achieve the pre-sale numbers they need to get finance. As each stage is readied for sale, purchase prices may be pushed up to give potential buyers the impression that prices are rising. This is nonsense, because until the property is sold by the first purchaser, it has never been sold, only bought, and it is extremely difficult to estimate the market value of such properties.

Nevertheless, if you find a new development where the first properties are being pre-sold off the plan at apparently discounted prices to obtain some initial sales, you may get a bargain. There are some risks with this form of property investment that don't occur in others: the first is that the developer, builder or a major contractor may go out of business before the project is complete. This can cause significant delays, unanticipated structural or design changes to the finished product and maybe even loss of your invested funds. The second risk is related to the nature of boom markets — they can change much more quickly than other markets, so that the market may slow down or even bust before you can sell, leaving you caught short with an investment that is worth far less than what you have paid for it.

Hunt for bargains in stressed and buyer markets

Because booms don't last long you should have a strategy waiting in the wings for those times when prices are falling, such as in buyer or even stressed markets, and when they are neutral, but with no prospect of growth in sight. Investing in such markets is completely different to the others because it relies on creating value from negotiating a low sale price rather than building value or waiting for passive growth to start again. It is an unfortunate fact that after a period of rapidly rising interest rates, tight housing finance and falling prices, a number of owners find themselves in trouble and unable to manage their repayments. Others are forced to sell because of work commitments or changing family circumstances, so there are always bargains to be found. Some of these desperate vendors will part with properties for a fraction of their real value because they have no choice but to sell.

While I don't endorse predatory buying practices, there are opportunities to make a blanket offer to all vendors in such markets on a 'take it or leave it' approach and there will usually be one or two who will accept because it is the only offer they receive. Other options are to check for mortgagee in-possession auction sales authorised by lenders because they only seek the amount financed, not the value of the property. Narrowing down your search in such areas involves locating suburbs or towns that your research, as shown Key 2, indicates to be buyer or stressed markets. You then narrow down your search to concentrate on localities where buyers most at risk have been active. Table 4.5 shows you what these are and where to find them.

Table 4.5: finding areas with stressed owners

Type of property loan	Location	Years since purchase
First house purchase	New outer suburban development	1–2
First unit purchase	Growth corridor development	1–2
Discretionary second purchase	Holiday or resort location	2–4
Off the plan investment	Off the plan with rental guarantee	3–5
Speculative investment	Infrastructure or new mining town	5+

First-home buyers

Lenders know that the period of greatest risk for home loan defaults is in the first year or two of a first-home buyer loan. The borrowers may have over-anticipated their expected income, or they may have overspent on furniture and fittings, interest rates may start to rise or economic conditions could worsen. The major cause of early sales in such areas is family breakups caused by the stress that owning a first home in worsening conditions presents. However, if the borrowers can get through this potential crisis period and maintain their repayments they'll tend to hang on. This is because it is now their home. Owner-occupied new developments therefore present the greatest opportunity for finding bargains in this critical early period.

Discretionary purchases

The second group of potentially stressed owners is comprised of people who make a discretionary property purchase of a holiday house or unit in a popular beachside or mountain resort. This is usually done during economic boom times, and if economic or financial conditions deteriorate, it is the first asset to go. These are often located in areas desired by retirees, who are immune to such economic downturns, so the opportunity is there to pick up a bargain from a stressed owner and then sell it in a few years to a retiree couple.

Off-the-plan and speculative investment

The two other groups of potentially stressed owners are investors. Many investors, especially those located overseas who have no access to on-the-ground information, may buy off-the-plan units for far more than they are really worth, relying on rental guarantees and glossy promises of future price-growth potential. They are often forced to sell when the rental guarantee period expires and the rents they receive suddenly drop dramatically, or disappear altogether while the property is vacant.

You can time these opportunities by narrowing down your search within suburbs where rental surpluses exist (as explained in Key 2) and then look for projects where the rental guarantees are about to end. If you notice a dramatic rise in the number of advertised rental vacancies, you will also start to see properties placed on the market by disillusioned investors, needing to sell because they can't maintain the loan repayments. In some severe cases, such as in Queensland's Gold Coast unit market in 2008 to 2010, the oversupply of rental stock followed by surplus stock on the market led to falls of over 40 per cent in median unit prices. The other investor-created stressed markets are created by speculative purchases — those made in expectation of a new infrastructure project, port development or mine expansion that either does not occur or does not have the anticipated effect on housing demand. While some early investors may have made huge profits during the confidence-building stages, it is the last investors in such markets who suffer the most.

How to find the next potential boom market

Most of the strategies already covered demonstrate the need to narrow down your search within a suburb or town, because there will always be pockets that have more potential than others. It is only when an entire city becomes a boom market that it sweeps everything before it, from houses to units of all sizes and in all locations, but even then there will be some areas that outperform others, because there will still be different types of housing markets providing various levels of growth potential. Key 1 shows you what they are, and Key 2 shows you how to find them.

There are also certain housing markets that can provide both high cash flow and the sort of capital growth sought by speculative investors. These typically start booming because of a local rise in rental demand that is followed by:

➤ investors moving in

➤ owner-occupiers buying

➤ developers providing more supply, and sometimes an oversupply.

This process takes many years to unwind, so that investors at the start will obtain the benefits of high rent growth as well as price-growth. Because the process starts with a rise in rental demand, we need to look at the opportunity-seekers described in Key 3 to see which type of renter might be the catalyst. They might be:

➤ workers moving to a captive rental market seeking high incomes

➤ students living away from home in university towns

➤ casual workers seeking easy work and a relaxing, entertaining lifestyle in tourist resorts.

This last group of opportunity seekers offers the most benefit to housing investors. Every year we receive nearly two and a half million overseas tourists and they bring their money with them, each spending an average of $2500 during their stay.

They pump more than $6 billion into the economies of the areas they visit, on:

➤ travel

➤ accommodation

➤ dining

➤ tours

➤ entertainment

➤ souvenirs.

This activity also stimulates local housing markets in the process but, although local communities receive most of the economic benefits of tourism, the housing booms they create are available to investors everywhere. To gain the biggest benefits from housing investment, we simply need to know which locations tourists are likely to visit in future.

While interstate and local tourists tend to favour the same holiday locations from one generation to the next, this is not the case with overseas tourists. Tourism Australia research shows that the destinations they prefer vary widely according to their countries of origin, and that we are about to receive a massive lift in tourist arrivals from China. By identifying the locations where they will stay, we can invest in properties before the booms start and reap the biggest rewards.

Table 4.6 shows how the main industries in a typical rural community both diversify and expand from dependence on one main primary industry to several new industries as tourist markets emerge and then become established.

Table 4.6: tourism creates job diversity and economic growth

Locality	Industry of employment	Percentage of workforce	Size of workforce
Rural location	Agriculture, forestry, fishing	25%	250
	Education services	5%	50
	Retail trade	5%	50
	All other industries		1000
Emerging tourist market	Accommodation	10%	300
	Restaurants and food services	7%	210
	Agriculture, forestry, fishing	4%	120
	Retail trade	4%	120
	All other industries		3000
Established tourist market	Accommodation	25%	1500
	Restaurants and food services	13%	750
	Scenic and sightseeing tours	6%	375
	Clothing and personal accessories retailing	4%	240
	All other industries		6000

Source: QuickStats 2006, 2011, Australian Bureau of Statistics.

As a result of these new tourist-related job-creation ventures, such as accommodation, restaurants, tours and entertainment, there is a flow-on effect that engages the whole community, leading to more employment and new businesses in the construction, retail and supply chain industries. In fact, according to the Bureau of Tourism Research Australia, the demand for new jobs can be up to three times the number of tourist arrivals during tourism booms.

Although some local or interstate tourists may take holiday lettings, the vast majority of overseas tourists do not. They holiday in resorts, hotels, hostels or camping areas and caravan parks so there is little direct increased demand for housing in locations where they visit. On the other hand, the rapid rise in the range and number of employment and new business opportunities created by tourist booms has a direct effect on housing demand. Investors can monitor and take advantage of these imminent housing booms because they can easily identify how, where and when they are likely to take place.

Locating the next tourism-related housing boom

Holiday resorts and retreats are located in the most interesting and desirable parts of our country, and tourism is a labour-intensive industry. It offers part-time and casual employment suiting younger people from larger towns and cities who are already attracted to such coastal and country tourist areas for the lifestyle. When the number of tourists to an area starts to rise, one of the first noticeable effects on housing is that the growth in rental demand quickly exceeds the number of tourist arrivals because of the arrival of these young opportunity seekers. The rise in rental demand is closely followed by an increase in demand for owner-occupied housing generated by the owners and managers of new business enterprises.

The growth in diversity and availability of recreational and entertainment facilities also attracts more local and interstate tourists. Some of these holidaymakers are then tempted to buy a holiday home, investment property or future retirement retreat. As the demand for both rentals and owner-occupied properties continues to rise the area comes under the notice of developers who may see opportunities to build medium- to high-rise unit developments and house and land packages on new housing estates. These are predominantly marketed to future retirees and investors and, as the popularity of the locality grows, project marketers will sell many of these as off-the-plan investments to overseas buyers.

This last stage is often the period of greatest sales in the life cycle of a tourism location, and it often occurs when the tourist boom is declining and real demand is falling. Such a sequence of events took place in the Gold Coast housing market, starting from 2000–01 with strong housing price and rent growth, until the onset of the Global Financial Crisis in 2008–09 saw both retiree and overseas investor numbers fall dramatically. The resultant oversupply of high-rise units reached chronic proportions in the following years and may take several more to recover.

Yet the Gold Coast has experienced several past housing booms and busts, as have many other holiday and resort locations. One of the main reasons for this is that overseas tourists tend to favour destinations that best meet their needs for a perfect holiday and, as the numbers of tourists from different countries has changed, so have their preferred destinations in Australia.

In years past, Australia was popular with tourists from Japan, the USA and Europe for specific reasons such as:

➤ honeymoon locations

➤ the Outback

➤ the Great Barrier Reef

➤ golf courses

➤ fly-fishing

➤ big game fishing

➤ casinos

➤ theme parks

➤ the opportunity to enjoy opulent, luxurious accommodation and dining at comparatively low prices.

This led to the creation of resorts specifically designed to cater for these needs, stretching all the way from Tarraleah in southern Tasmania to the Port Douglas Mirage Resort in northern Queensland.

The falling away of tourist numbers to such locations in recent years has been due to a combination of the high Aussie dollar and post–Global Financial Crisis economic recessions in Japan and the USA. The Bureau of Tourism Research has conducted in-depth surveys to ascertain not only where overseas tourists have come from in the past but where they are likely to come from in future. The results indicate that while the numbers of tourists from Japan and the USA are not likely to return to their pre–Global Financial Crisis boom levels in the near future, the number of tourists from China is already rising dramatically and that, by 2020, the number of yearly Chinese tourist arrivals will exceed 1.5 million.

Over half of the expected Chinese tourist arrivals will be aged under 35, and three-quarters will come from the cities of Shanghai, Beijing and Guangzhou. The populations of these three huge cities total nearly three times that of Australia, and comprise many of China's rapidly growing aspiring and current middle-class residents. They work and live in some of the most densely urbanised cities in the world and so when they go on holidays, they prefer something quite different — natural environments and locations with unspoilt world-class beauty that are safe and easily accessible. The priorities that drew tourists from the UK, Europe, USA and Japan are at the bottom of their list.

Armed with this understanding of what Chinese tourists look for when visiting Australia, we can easily see why certain locations are becoming more popular and why some holiday spots are missing altogether from the list shown in table 4.7.

Table 4.7: most popular Chinese tourist destinations

Location	Percentage of Chinese visitors
Sydney	57%
Gold Coast	55%
Tropical North Queensland	44%
Melbourne	23%
Kangaroo Island	22%
Margaret River	18%
Red Centre	17%
Byron Bay	15%
Kakadu	13%

Source: Chinese Visitor Survey, Bureau of Tourism Research, Department of Foreign Affairs and Trade.

This destination list demonstrates the popularity of different Australian places with Chinese tourists and indicates where tourism is likely to grow as an industry according to the expected rise in the number of Chinese tourists. While it would seem that such a list of the most popular locations solves our quest to find potential tourist-led boom areas, there are still a few issues. Some of the destinations shown in table 4.7 are capital cities such as Sydney and Melbourne, and a rapid increase in overseas tourist arrivals is not likely to have any effect on housing prices in those cities. Destinations in the Red Centre and Kakadu are not suitable for private housing investors as there are no freehold properties in the major support towns such as Yulara and Jabiru. Tasmania's popularity stems from the Cradle Mountain–Lake St Clair National Park where accommodation for both employees and tourists is provided. As the nearest sizable city is Devonport, 80 kilometres to the north, it is difficult to assess what impact, if any, overseas tourism will have. The Gold Coast is still recovering from a spate of high-rise unit overdevelopment and reduced housing demand, but the Coast's high popularity with Chinese tourists indicates that another tourist-led housing market boom is not too far away.

To find locations with imminent tourist-led housing boom potential, we need to limit our search to those towns that already have small resident populations and are in the most favoured Chinese tourist destinations shown in table 4.7 (see p. 115). Some of these will be emerging tourist towns, such as Margaret River in Western Australia and Kangaroo Island in South Australia, where well over 10 per cent of the local working population is employed in tourism-related industries, but the main industries are still farming and horticulture. Others will be transitional tourist towns in the Whitsundays and far north Queensland, where entrepreneurs are refurbishing and re-opening old lavish resorts that were built for a previous generation of tourists from Japan and the USA, updating them to styles preferred by Chinese visitors. These locations are shown in table 4.8. Because our research has shown that the first boom signs in such towns will be shortages of rental properties and high rental demand, we have tested the rental market to ensure we are selecting towns with the highest growth potential.

Table 4.8: locations where tourism will have the biggest potential effect

Location	Town or city	Current population	Investor-owned dwellings	Rental vacancies	Percentage vacant
Tropical North Queensland	Airlie Beach–Cannonvale	8000	1600	120	8%
	Port Douglas–Mossman	5800	1180	76	6%
Kangaroo Island, SA	Kingscote	2100	260	14	5%
Byron Bay, NSW	Byron Bay	5000	820	36	4%
Margaret River, WA	Margaret River	5500	700	20	3%

Source: QuickStats 2006, 2011, Australian Bureau of Statistics; International Visitor Survey, Bureau of Tourism Research, DFAT; and Property Power Database, Property Power Partners.

The towns shown in table 4.8 have all the right growth dynamics in place right now and they are where significant rises in the numbers of tourists will put almost immediate pressure on rents and then prices. By investing in such locations we can enjoy the successive housing growth waves caused by overseas tourism, retiree buyers and investors, then sell before the boom slows down. To narrow down your search in such locations you only need to consider where workers in the local tourism industry are likely to live, which will almost invariably be in low-maintenance units or houses close to the town centres. As the tourist market matures and retirees start to move to the area, you will find that they prefer to buy the same types of properties in the same inner locations and will provide you with excellent opportunities to maximise your investment return by selling to them. In other words, avoid high-maintenance houses with large backyards and areas located away from town, or all the high returns you anticipate may not eventuate.

You can see that the method used to narrow down your search depends on the type of housing market and what stage of growth or decline it is in. Each of these housing investment strategies is highly successful if used at the right time. This means that we must be flexible enough to change our strategy to suit the market, not ignore the market because it doesn't suit our strategy.

How to conduct your own online research

From the desktop analysis methods you have used in the previous keys, you should have a good idea of:

➤   your property price range

➤   the type of preferred property

➤ its probable location

➤ how the property is going to meet your investment goals.

Before you can narrow down your search to specific properties and start searching for them, you need to be certain about the localities that will best meet your needs, and much of this research can be conducted using the internet.

You can Google sites that feature the area such as local government and tourism sites. Discover what makes the area tick. What do most people do for a living? Get a feel for the area. Research its:

➤ location

➤ local industry

➤ recreation

➤ local climate

➤ retail, commercial and education facilities

➤ transport.

Use www.googleearth.com to check what the information is telling you. While using Google Earth, make sure that you have enabled the 'borders, labels and roads' layers so that you get a better feel for the area. You can see the shopping and industrial centres, and recent housing developments show up clearly, as do infrastructure developments such as new roads and railways. Keep in mind the dates of the aerial mapping—they are usually not more than a year old. In this way you can compare what the promotional sites, estate agents and developers are telling you to what you can see for yourself. When you look for listed properties that may meet your criteria, keep Google Earth open so that you can check their location.

Conduct on-the-ground research

When your initial research is finished there's only one way to find out if any pieces of the puzzle are still missing, and that's by completing the picture with actual on-the-ground research. This is because housing market stats and your analysis of them can only provide part of the story, and even expert opinion may be based on false assumptions. Your own on-the-ground research can show you whether the published information is right or wrong and may give you new insights into the investment potential of an area that can't be obtained any other way.

On-the-ground research doesn't mean getting in your car and driving around the area, visiting real estate agents and asking them some questions about the local property market. Real estate agents are the last people to visit, and only when you have finished all your other avenues of on-the-ground research. Start with your own personal tour of inspection and drive through the local streets to check the general condition of properties and their presentation.

The following is not an exhaustive list, but shows you how to assess an area's housing market potential. Here is what to look for as you drive through an area:

➤ Is this a prosperous, go-ahead area with sidewalk cafes and alfresco dining?

➤ Is this area going nowhere with empty shops and faded 'to let' signs everywhere?

➤ Are people proud of their community, as evidenced by well-maintained lawns and gardens?

➤ Are there security issues, with gated communities and shuttered shop fronts?

➤ Are there social issues evidenced by charity outlets and employment agencies?

➤ Are there many 'for sale' signs in some streets, some of which are obviously old?

As mentioned on page 48, also check for signs of overdevelopment:

➤ Can you see any large vacant fenced-off land areas?

➤ Do some roads end abruptly but are obviously intended to go further in the future?

➤ Are there vacant shopping strips on main roads with no 'to let' signs?

➤ Have you noticed any blocks or groups of vacant, even derelict terraces or houses in an area with medium- to high-rise units?

These are all signs that developers own the land and that more housing will follow. In areas where housing demand and supply are in balance, the sheer weight of new stock numbers can lead to oversupplies. On the other hand, the nature of any new developments may rejuvenate an area and generate further demand for housing.

Seek the editor of the local paper if there is one and talk to officials at the local council office because the locals working there will usually be happy to talk about the latest housing developments and what is likely to drive demand for more housing. Only by asking questions about any possible or proposed developments, their size, type and timing, will you know their likely impact on the local housing market and your possible investment in it. While an increase in housing demand is usually a positive sign that prices may rise, proposed or possible new housing developments may lead to an oversupply. Here are some typical questions that you might ask local officials and townsfolk:

➤ Is the area adequately sewered?

➤ Is there town water?

➤ Are there ever any water restrictions?

➤ When, where and how serious was the last bushfire?

➤ When, where and how serious was the last flood?

➤ Have there been any other natural disasters?

➤ Where are the local trouble spots and what causes them?

➤ What sort of households are moving in and why?

➤ What sort of households are leaving and why?

➤ What are the major industries of employment?

➤ Are these industries thriving or struggling?

➤ Are there any plans for new industries?

You can ask whether people are moving into or out of the area to retire, or to work in a new infrastructure development project, mining expansion or tourism enterprise. Remember that any proposed infrastructure is only relevant in terms of the number of new residents it brings into the area, and during the construction phase they will probably be renters.

The local police are excellent providers of 'inside' information and if you can find the local postman, he or she will be able to inform you exactly where the good and bad streets are. The answers you receive from conducting on-the-ground research will either confirm that your desktop research is correct and enable you to proceed with confidence, or they will refute your findings, in which case you need to look elsewhere.

✦ ✦ ✦

This key showed you how to narrow down your search within a suburb or town to identify the locality and type of property with the greatest potential to deliver the results you want no matter what the market conditions are. The next key to the property market shows you how to decide what property to buy.

Key 5

Decide what to buy

The previous key showed you how to narrow down your search within a suburb or town to identify the locality and properties with the greatest potential to deliver the results you want. This key to the property market helps you decide what type of property to buy, which depends on whether you are seeking:

➤ active growth from renovations

➤ passive capital growth

➤ high cash flow.

Let's look at each of these in turn.

Where and what to renovate for the greatest profit potential

Imagine that you have shares in Woolworths and in an effort to improve their value you visit your local supermarket and paint the exterior. Not only is this unlikely to result in a rise in the price of your shares, it may land you in trouble with the authorities. Yet this is exactly what you can do with your own properties, because housing is the only asset whose value you can improve through your own efforts. Even when markets are flat with prices going nowhere, you can maximise the asking rent for your property and reduce the vacancy rate or raise your potential sale price. You do not need to change the structure of the building to achieve this, either, because simple cosmetic renovations can raise the market value of your property and also make it easier to rent or sell.

This is why almost all property owners consider renovation at some stage. It's a quick and fun way to add instant sale value to any property, and most of us have the time, money and skills to cosmetically improve a house or unit with some paint or landscaping. Buying a property for renovation, especially structural renovation, offers even greater opportunities for profit, but requires more experience and expertise and the risks are greater as well. Delays and cost blowouts from unexpected approval requirements, unreliable sub-contractors or bad weather can really test the skill, budget and patience of the serious renovator. The purpose of this book is not to show you how to overcome such issues, as there are many excellent renovation publications and courses out there, but how to pick the best possible location. Here again, the common wisdom is to buy in a suburb with high price differential, and also in a street with high price differential, but many of the reports I have seen that provide this sort of information ignore the reasons why such variations occur and can lead renovators astray. For example, you may find from a renovation report that a street has a large difference in sale prices, which is a good thing for renovation potential. It can mean that if you can buy a property in a street at the lower end of the price range, you have only to do the improvements to achieve the higher end. Unfortunately, these sorts of reports may not show you why the difference in price is so great, and this may have nothing to do with the type of dwelling, but the fact that:

➤ some properties have a view that others don't

➤ one end of the street is near the local cemetery or a noisy night spot

➤ one side of the street occasionally floods

➤ some houses are nearer to a busy freeway, and so on.

While part of the answer to this dilemma is to do some on-the-ground research and take a look, it is also essential to decide whether you are going to rent the renovated property to tenants, or place it on the market as soon as the work is done. This is because the types of households who generate the most rental demand in the suburb or town where you are investing may be very different to the types of households who will generate the highest buyer demand — and this in turn should help you to determine not only what type of renovation will be most effective, but where your property should be located within the suburb or town. Some localities will have far higher renovation potential than others, and knowing how to find them can help you get the best result from your renovation project.

Select areas with high passive growth potential

Even when all goes well, many successful renovators discover that the price they expected or needed to realise from the property's sale turns out to be far lower than they expected, while others find that the sale price is much higher. This is usually because the upper price limits of the other properties in a street, locality or suburb control the ultimate value of any renovation and because the potential value of properties continuously changes in accordance with supply and demand. Table 5.1 shows how this often happens, much to the surprise of the renovators concerned.

Table 5.1: what went wrong and what went right?

	What went wrong?	What went right?
Suburb	Highett	Essendon West
Purchase price	$550 000	$550 000
Median price	$718 000	$660 000
Hold period	1 year	1 year
Expected added value	$250 000	$250 000
Expected sale price	$800 000	$800 000
Reno, hold and sale costs	$100 000	$100 000
Actual added value	$150 000	$250 000
Price movement during hold	−10%	17%
Passive growth or correction	−$55 000	$93 500
Actual sale price	$645 000	$893 500
	Ozden's net loss −$5000	Jen's net profit $243 500

Some time ago, Ozden bought a house for renovation in the Melbourne suburb of Highett and Jen bought in a similar type of suburb, Essendon West. Each paid $550 000 for their property and spent $100 000 on buying, holding, selling and renovation costs, expecting to lift their property's value by $250 000. A year later, Ozden's sale resulted in a net loss of $5000 and he vowed never to renovate again. Jen, on the other hand walked away with $243 000 from the sale of her Essendon West property and is busy on her next renovation project.

Both of them did everything by the book, so how could such unexpected outcomes occur? The answer is that house prices in Highett fell by nearly 10 per cent during Ozden's hold period, and the fall in demand was greatest in the very type of house that he was renovating. Over the same time, house prices in Essendon West rose by 17 per cent and resulted in high demand for Jen's renovated property when it went to auction. This was the only difference between Jen's triumph and Ozden's disaster.

Renovators will be selling a different property to the one they purchased. The aim is to renovate to the style of property and price range in the street and the suburb that is sought by most buyers in the area. The key is to renovate to the most desired buying price, not from it.

Your initial desktop research should establish not just current prices for the property being purchased, but expected demand for the property being sold using the methods outlined in Key 2 — something Jen did very well and Ozden failed to do at all. It is also important to check that there are sufficient numbers of stock available on the market of the type of dwelling that you will be renovating from. Renovation is becoming extremely popular and if there are only a limited number of suitable properties in a certain locality, renovators tend to bid against each other to make a purchase, defeating the purpose.

When it's time to sell, you are looking for a seller market with large numbers of potential buyers and few similar properties listed for sale. You need to renovate to meet the expected demand — and this means putting yourself in the shoes of your potential purchasers and researching their preferences. Some areas have stocks of properties just waiting for renovation, and high demand for the finished product, but where can you find such gems?

Select properties with active growth potential

Properties with high active growth potential are often hiding away in some of the most desirable locations of our major cities. In particular, they are ex–holiday homes, ex–housing commission homes and older dwellings in neglected inner suburbs.

Ex–holiday homes

Ex–holiday homes are scattered all along the coastal, bayside, riverside and mountain fringes of our major cities and regional areas. Once spurned as second-rate accommodation for battlers, these homes are often located in the best parts of desirable suburbs, usually on large blocks of land, and your improvement of them will be welcomed both by the neighbours and the local council. Although they are a limited and rapidly diminishing housing renovation opportunity, numbers of them still exist in areas surprisingly close to our urban centres. As figure 5.1 shows, they present enormous potential for renovators.

Figure 5.1: renovating ex-holiday homes

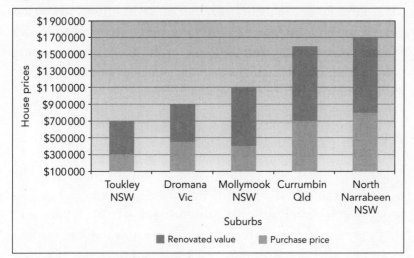

Source: Australian Property Monitors house price data adapted from *Australian Property Investor* Databank.

The main benefits are their highly sought-after locations, while the main drawback is that many were built on the cheap with whatever materials and labour were available locally. An inspection of the following elements is essential:

➤ footings

➤ roofing

➤ wiring

➤ plumbing

➤ drainage.

Many cheapies survive on the coastal outskirts of our major cities and beyond, where the renovated properties are bought by retirees, but ex–holiday homes occasionally pop up for sale in well-established, highly sought-after suburbs. These renovated homes appeal to aspirational homeowners who want to live in prestigious locations and they present enormous value-adding potential for renovators, because they can be renovated to suit the preferences of current buyers.

Housing commission estates

Our capital cities and regional centres contain many suburbs with substantial stock of current and former housing commission estates, mostly built during the 1950s, 1960s and 1970s in outlying areas, many of which are now well-established locations, such as Sydney's beachside suburbs, Melbourne's outer bayside and Mornington Peninsula suburbs and Hobart's Eastern Shore. Most of the houses are now privately owned, having been refurbished and renovated, and the suburbs have been gentrified. Pockets of the original homes remain, well-located but tucked away between much grander homes, and it is here that the opportunities for renovators lie.

Figure 5.2 shows the opportunities that these homes offer renovators, as they are mostly well constructed and, although of modest nature, often situated on large blocks of land.

Figure 5.2: renovating ex–housing commission homes

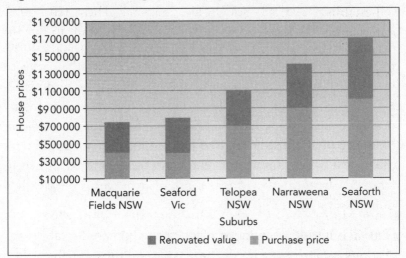

Source: Australian Property Monitors house price data adapted from *Australian Property Investor* Databank.

There are also clusters of ex- (and current-) housing commission estates located in close proximity to large industrial complexes such as those in Newcastle and Wollongong, near Western Port Bay in Victoria and the northern suburbs of Adelaide around the satellite city of Elizabeth. Some of these are undergoing a process of gentrification, while others are still entirely comprised of houses as they were originally built. The areas with the greatest opportunities are those where the process of renewal and refurbishment is underway, but not yet complete.

Old inner suburban houses

Renovation opportunities are greatest where there is a large variety of property types and prices, and nowhere is this more prevalent than in the older surviving inner suburban ring of houses that constituted the entire metropolitan area of our cities a hundred years ago. Not only are these houses located in highly desirable areas, some have not been improved for a generation or longer and their seemingly endless variation of styles and sizes offer great opportunities for renovators. The suburbs shown in figure 5.3 are located in inner suburban areas with a huge variety of housing styles and prices.

Figure 5.3: renovating older inner urban homes

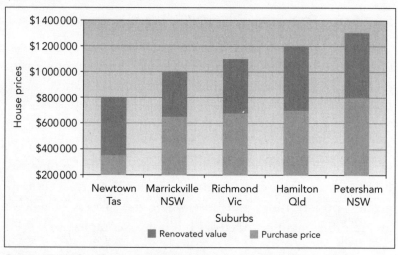

Source: Australian Property Monitors house price data adapted from *Australian Property Investor* Databank.

In the postwar years, houses in such inner suburbs were looked down on by the locals as colonial or Federation relics and this enabled migrant families, particularly in Sydney and Melbourne, to buy them relatively cheaply and set up the ethnic communities for which they are now famous. These suburbs have become, or are in the process of becoming, rejuvenated precincts sought by professional couples who enjoy the vibrant sidewalk café lifestyle and their cosmopolitan atmosphere. The type of demand dictates the types of houses that can best be renovated, the locations and the way in which they should be renovated. While there is great variety of housing styles in older inner suburbs, unless a house can be easily renovated to the appropriate living style, it will not achieve the desired result.

The only way to maximise your returns from renovation is to find and buy properties that will enable you to obtain two uplifts in price — one through your own efforts and the other from passive growth.

Is the property right for passive growth?

Having used the keys to the property market up to this stage, you should have a good idea of the type of property you are interested in and where it is likely to be located. Now is the time to visit local estate agents and see how many listings and lettings they have and how many have 'sold' stickers. Although they are usually area experts, agents will often put a positive spin on what they tell you, which is only natural, as they are in the business of selling. You shouldn't visit them until you have a list of questions to ask about the area as well as properties you are interested in inspecting. You can ask them who is buying properties, which areas are most popular and what types of dwellings sell quickly. Here are some examples of the sorts of questions to ask real estate agents:

➤ What sort of households are moving in and why?

➤ What sort of households are leaving and why?

➤ What types of homes are most in demand?

➤ What types of households are on their wait list?

➤ What changes if any have they noticed in the numbers and types of renters over the last year?

➤ Where are the local spots that attract troublesome renters and why?

➤ Where are the local trouble spots and what causes them?

➤ What are the major industries of employment?

➤ Are these industries thriving or struggling?

➤ Are there any plans for new industries?

Is the property right for rental growth?

This is the question most investors fail to ask or, if they do, ask the wrong people. Cash flow is about enjoying high rental demand for your property and comes from the households that rent in the area. These are usually not questions to ask the real estate agent, but to keep for the property manager when you return to the agency. Families want homes with large backyards near schools, shops and bus stops; young couples look for low-maintenance, attractive living near recreation and entertainment facilities; new overseas arrivals want access to public transport and employment; and older couples prefer single-storey living away from busy or noisy streets.

It is the type of households who make up most of the renters that decide which properties have the greatest rental demand and where they are located, so you need to find out from the right people: property managers. Here are the sorts of questions you can ask property managers:

➤ What types of homes are most in demand?

➤ What types of households typically rent in the suburb?

➤ What types of properties and locations do these households prefer?

➤ How long are typical lease periods?

➤ What are the vacancy rates?

➤ What are the average vacancy periods between lettings?

➤ How many prospective tenants are on their wait list?

➤ What types of households are on their wait list?

➤ What changes if any have they noticed in the types of renters over the last year?

➤ Where are the local spots with troublesome rentals and why?

When you've completed your on-the-ground research in this logical and comprehensive manner, you will have confirmed or refuted the numbers and filled in the gaps to make the best possible investment choice. On the cost side, you should have a good idea of the:

➤ rates

➤ body corporate fees

➤ building insurance

➤ property management fees.

While a building and pest inspection is usually essential, your personal inspection of a property will reveal which repairs are visibly essential and those that are only desirable.

On the income side, you should know what the current rent for the property is and its rental history.

Some issues with a property may be obvious, such as the presence of noisy or unruly neighbours, but others will need your close inspection to reveal themselves, so when you have decided making an offer, first ask the real estate agent showing you the property why it is for sale and what issues there are with the property: agents have both a legal and moral obligation to tell you if they know of any issues, but only if asked.

This key showed you what type of property to buy according to your goals for passive growth, cash flow or renovation potential and the next key shows you how to make sure you pay no more than the right price.

Key 6

Determine how much to pay

Key 5 showed you how to find the right property, and this key shows you how to determine the right price for that property. It also gives you an insight into the various ways that property values are determined in the market. If prospective vendors are aware that demand is higher than supply they may:

➤ encourage buyers to compete against each other

➤ refuse to discount

➤ insist on excessively ambitious asking prices

➤ use sales processes such as auctions to drive prices up.

In addition, if there are few listings in an area, it can be difficult for buyers to know a property's fair market value. The problem is that if you pay too much, you are handing some of your profit to the seller and will not achieve the desired level of growth. You may not even achieve any growth at all, so paying no more than market value is an essential step in successful investment.

Many investors think that property has intrinsic value and that this is determined by the value of the land itself. Others believe that the value of property is set purely by the demand for it, which is in turn determined by:

➤ the location of the property

➤ the size of the house or unit

➤ the number of bedrooms, bathrooms, garage spaces

➤ its aspect

➤ its proximity to facilities and services.

In fact, there are hundreds of such different attributes that give a property its value, but before we can determine what any property is worth, we need to answer the question: does land have inherent worth?

What gives land its value?

I was chatting with a fellow hiker in the Tasmanian highlands who had just made a significant land purchase. Bursting with excitement, she told me 'I've just bought ten hectares of land for each of my five grandchildren!'

'How very thoughtful — what did that set you back?' I asked.

'Just $20 a hectare, and each block has unbelievable views!'

This seemed an incredible bargain, so I asked her, 'Wow! Where did you find such a fantastic investment?'

'On the moon.' she replied.

It was true. She showed me the title deeds she had received from the vendor, an internet-based company called Lunar Embassy, whose business is selling lunar land. Each impressive-looking title document detailed the exact location of each grandchild's plot of lunar land.

'They're certainly very innovative property marketers.' I said.

'I think it's an ideal gift for my grandchildren, as one day, who knows how much moon land could be worth!'

This story illustrates the notion that land has intrinsic value no matter where it is located. The belief is rooted deep in our past, beginning when we ceased being hunter gatherers and settled into farming communities. The control of land enabled us to house, feed and raise families in peace. Land ownership is synonymous with security and this explains why property is fundamentally different to other forms of investment. While you can buy shares, savings, bonds or commodities without any guarantee of a return, everyone needs a place to live and every home requires land, so wherever there are people, property has some value. The lunar land venture shows us that this concept is so thoroughly entrenched in our psyches that people will even buy land on the moon in the hope that it will have value sometime in the future.

Taken to extremes, this belief can create land booms driven by speculation, where the demand is fuelled purely by buyers who believe there will be more demand from other buyers and that prices will rise as a result. Such price rises have nothing to do with the use to which the land is put (representing its real value), but are about the notion that demand alone is sufficient to make a good investment.

The most graphic example of such a land boom contains valuable lessons for all investors today, even though it occurred well over a hundred years ago. It was back in the 1870s and 1880s, when people were flush with money from the gold rush years and Australia's population was increasing rapidly. Formerly small settlements such as Sydney, Melbourne and Brisbane were becoming prosperous cities. Wealth was generated from wool, wheat, timber and mineral exports as the hinterland was opened up, new ports were constructed and railways spread outwards to new rural markets.

One of the proposed railway routes was across the Blue Mountains in New South Wales, where one acre (nearly half a hectare) of land in the 1870s was worth $2 in today's money. When the railway plans were made public, a frenzy of land subdivisions and sales ensued, with speculators buying blocks in the expectation that they would be near the railway line, or even better, near one of the proposed stations, such as Katoomba. Newly subdivided land prices quickly rose from $100 each in 1883 to $800 in 1886, sold off the plan in auctioneers' rooms in Sydney. Undeveloped and unserviced, the blocks were then sold and resold again to other investors until by 1889 land prices topped $1600 per block — more than two years' average income at the time and mostly on borrowed money. In 1890 the British banks cut lending to the Australian colonies and their economies crashed. The demand for land stopped, everyone tried to sell at once and prices quickly collapsed. Figure 6.1 shows what happened to Katoomba's land prices when the crash occurred.

Figure 6.1: the Katoomba land boom and bust 1883–1892

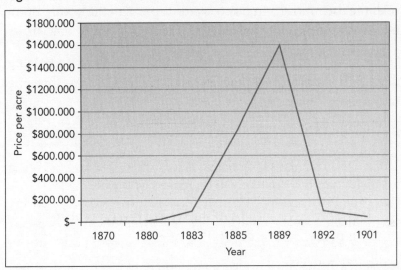

Source: Australian National Library's online Trove facility; Mitchell Library archives.

Disappointment quickly turned to panic as everyone tried to get out at the same time, and by 1892 the price of a block of land had dropped back to the 1883 pre-boom level of $100. Prices continued to slide further to just $50 per block in 1901 and then didn't rise for another twenty years.

The lesson for us all from the Katoomba land boom is that land value can arise from two different types of demand. If the need for housing in a suburb or town is growing and leads to a shortage, then prices or rents are likely to rise in response to the demand. Even if demand slows, prices are unlikely to crash because the demand is genuine. Housing investments made in such areas are low risk and highly secure because they are based on the function of land as providing homes. But when demand is pushed along by speculative investment, prices will rise only for as long as the number of investors trying to buy exceeds the number who want to sell. Reading property values in such markets is tricky and can result in heavy losses by investors who mistime their move and buy towards the end of the boom, or try to sell after the bubble has burst.

To avoid such disasters, investors should look at the underlying demand dynamics of any housing market where they are thinking of investing. These are:

➤ the number of new households moving into a suburb or locality

➤ whether they are likely to be renters or buyers

➤ the shortage or surplus of the type of dwellings they will prefer.

Never justify the price of a property purchase just because others are investing there — you may as well buy land on the moon. Having established that the value of land is determined by the demand for dwellings built on it, how can we accurately measure the value of these properties?

The median sale price can be misleading

One of the basic measures of housing values is the median sale price of houses or units in a suburb. This is the figure you see quoted in press releases and property reports that gives us an indication of house or unit prices in a suburb and tells us whether they have gone up or down. The median price is often used as a guide to the price of a particular property in a suburb because we can compare its attributes to those that make up the majority of homes in the suburb. For example, if most homes in the suburb are three-bedroom houses with one bathroom and no garage, and the median sale price for houses in the suburb is $500 000, then a three-bedroom house with one bathroom and no garage in the suburb should be worth about $500 000. A similar house with a view or in a better location in the suburb might be valued higher and a smaller house with no view would be worth less than $500 000. In other words, the suburb's median sale price can be used as a benchmark to value other properties in the area.

The median is the middle sale price when all the sale prices are ranked in order from highest to lowest. It can give us the wrong impression about property values in a suburb because the average time between sales for Australian property is fifteen years. This means that a completely different set of house or unit sales is being measured every month to create that month's median sale price. As a result it can change quite significantly in areas where newly built properties are being sold at prices that are higher or lower than the older existing stock. In other words, the median sale price can change because different properties are being sold, rather than because of changes in the median sale price of existing properties. Table 6.1 (overleaf) shows how recently published sale price data may lead you to believe that prices for the same types of properties in the listed suburbs fell dramatically during 2014, which was the year this analysis was made.

Table 6.1: a dramatic fall in the suburb's median sale price

Suburb	State	Current median sale price	Change in one year	Change in last three months
West Gladstone—units	Qld	$280000	−40%	−40%
Dural—units	NSW	$355000	−42%	−37%
Derby—houses	WA	$425000	−25%	−34%
Whyalla Stuart—houses	SA	$145000	−27%	−27%
Bombala—houses	NSW	$131000	−40%	−17%
Strahan—houses	Tas	$190000	−22%	−16%

Source: Australian Property Monitors house price data adapted from *Australian Property Investor* Databank and Property Power Database, Property Power Partners.

A closer examination of actual sales in the last three months of 2014 reveals that most of these were for smaller dwellings than those that had sold earlier, such as townhouses or villas instead of houses, and loft or studio apartments in lieu of one- and two-bedroom units. While drops in prices for the same types of dwelling may also have taken place, this is obscured by the overall fall in the median sale price. In fact, any reduction in the median price of more than 15 per cent over a three-month period should be treated with suspicion, as this is highly unlikely to be due purely to price movement.

In table 6.2 we notice the exact opposite effect on median housing prices due largely to the release of bigger and better properties on the market during 2014.

Table 6.2: a dramatic rise in the suburb's median sale price

Suburb	State	Current median sale price	Change in one year
Lavender Bay—units	NSW	$1 153 000	89%
Crafers West—houses	SA	$820 000	64%
Hilbert—houses	WA	$640 000	181%
Kin Kin—houses	Qld	$445 000	42%
Mount Macedon—houses	Vic	$811 000	35%
Coles Bay—houses	Tas	$465 000	47%

Source: Australian Property Monitors house price data adapted from Australian Property Investor Databank and Property Power Database, Property Power Partners.

In Lavender Bay, for example, new well-appointed units with superb Sydney Harbour views resulted in a median price hike of 80 per cent in one year but unit values in the suburb can vary from $500 000 to over $3 million.

The median sale price jumps around according to which properties have been sold recently. The only certainty we can derive from the median sale price in suburbs such as Lavender Bay is that the median price rise was caused more by sales of different types of properties than it was by a rise in price for the same types of properties. This issue with the median price is likely to be more pronounced in areas where new developments are taking place and the new stock is substantially different from the older existing stock. They include outer suburban housing estates, inner urban precincts and growth corridors with medium- and high-density unit developments. These sorts of issues with the median sale price have led analysts to adopt other methods of estimating what properties are worth.

How analysts estimate property values

Property analysts have come up with some innovative methods of solving the issue of different properties having been sold each time the median sale price is measured. One is to use the difference in sale price each time the same property is sold, which is called the repeat sales method. Because it can take about fifteen years on average for the same property to be sold again, this needs a huge database to gather the sale information of every property sold over time. It can't take into account any improvements that have been made to these properties between sales and, unless it takes inflation into account, is likely to severely undervalue properties.

To get around this, other analysts measure the changes in sale price that occur over time for the same types of properties, so that they end up with a set of median sale prices for dwellings based on their attributes and issue a median based on types of properties, which is called a *hedonic median*.

Still others use combinations of these methods, and this is why we end up with each data provider offering a different median price for houses or units for each suburb, and a different estimated value for any particular property. As a result, you may be tempted to use a free or paid property price report that you can obtain online from data providers, but some of these are no more than lead generation devices, and provide little more than a list of recent sales, the median price of properties in the suburbs, or even an estate agent's appraisal. While it is compulsory for an estate agent to provide an appraisal of a property's fair market value to their vendor (the seller), there is no obligation for them to do this for prospective buyers.

Real estate agents are generally quite accurate at estimating fair market value and will only attempt to raise vendor expectations if it is a sellers' market, or lower them if it is a buyers' market. This is because estate agents rely on turnover rather than price to achieve their commission and they will endeavour to set a price that is going to achieve a reasonably quick sale. Sometimes however, the asking price can be much lower than fair market value, especially in areas where there have been few recent comparable sales, and it can be higher when the vendor has unrealistic expectations and the agent has been unable to convince the vendor otherwise. You can either pay for a property price report from a recognised property market information provider or you can estimate the market value yourself, by using the same methods that sworn valuers do.

Make your own market value estimate

Sworn valuers compare the prices of recently sold properties to the property being valued using attributes such as:

➤ bedroom, bathroom and garage count

➤ floor area

➤ land area

➤ comparable condition

➤ location.

Using the same process, it is possible for you to create a reasonably accurate estimate of any property's value. A number of online services provide free property price estimate information such as:

➤ the average and median property price in any suburb or capital

➤ growth rates

➤ evidence of the highest and lowest recorded sales.

You can also find recent sale prices in the area from sites such as www.onthehouse.com.au. Many of these services are free and enable you to search for sale and rental listings by property, street or suburb. You can refine your search by date, price or property attributes, such as bedroom and bathroom counts. Always check that the source of information provided is genuine, that is, is sourced from government notified sales plus sales reported by estate agents.

There are several ways to use published data in the same way that a sworn valuer does, which will enable you to come up with an accurate market value estimate. Firstly, search for the most recent sales of the same property. Then make up a list of the price of all recent sales in the locality ranked by value (the more the better) and select the middle value. If the recent sales list has more than ten properties, shorten the list to about ten of the closest sales by location that have the same number of bedrooms and rank them by value, selecting the middle value, which is the median of nearby comparable sales.

Example of making your own estimate

Let's assume that you are interested in purchasing a property at 21 Bark Street, Standardville. The asking price is $450 000, but what is its fair market value? In Table 6.3 I have listed all recent nearby sales of three-bedroom properties, showing other details such as bathrooms and garage spaces, special obvious attributes, if any, and the condition of each property compared to the property I am considering. I have then ranked them by sale price from highest to lowest. This is exactly the same process that a sworn valuer undertakes when estimating the value of a property. The median, or middle ranked, property is at 7 Flower Street and sold for $430 000, which shows you that the fair market value of 21 Bark Street is $430 000 and that the asking price of $450 000 is slightly high.

Table 6.3: list of recent sales of comparable properties

Street address	Suburb	Bedrooms	Bathrooms	Garage spaces	Special attributes	Comparable condition	Sale price
8 Flower Street	Standardville	3	1	1	Ocean view	Superior	$500 000
2 Window Street	Standardville	3	2	2	Close to school	Superior	$470 000
34 Floor Ave	Standardville	3	2	2		Superior	$470 000
11 Gate Ave	Standardville	3	2	2		Similar	$470 000
7 Garage Street	Standardville	3	2	2	Near shops	Similar	$460 000
11 Shrub Street	Standardville	3	2	2		Similar	$460 000
3 Wall Lane	Standardville	3	2	2		Similar	$450 000
7 Flower Street	Standardville	3	2	2		Similar	$430 000
7 Window Street	Standardville	3	2	2	Close to school	Similar	$430 000
18 Path Ave	Standardville	3	2	2		Similar	$430 000
24 Tree Ave	Standardville	3	2	2		Inferior	$430 000
16 Kerb Street	Standardville	3	2	1		Inferior	$420 000
92 Gutter Lane	Standardville	3	2	1		Inferior	$420 000
8 Tree Ave	Standardville	3	1	1		Inferior	$410 000
7 Wall Lane	Standardville	3	1	1		Inferior	$400 000
4 Flower Street	Standardville	3	1	1		Needs work	$400 000
1 Fence Road	Standardville	3	1	0			$320 000

When you have determined an estimated fair market value for a property, you can then use online data provider services to obtain a free or paid estimate of the property's fair market value and compare it to your own estimate. It's not difficult to do this research — it can even be fun — and it's also essential. While the estimates you generate in this way are not replacements for a sworn valuation, they may well be more accurate than many property price estimate reports that cost money.

Making the offer

Having determined what the fair market value of the property is you can now make an offer, but there are a number of details you need to check before you do this:

➤ *Buyer's agent.* When you are ready to make an offer, you may wish to consider using a buyer's agent, particularly if it's a sellers' market and properties are selling quickly, or if your negotiation skills or techniques are not what you would want them to be. The fees for such services are usually a percentage of the price and are similar to those you pay when selling a property. The buyer's agent should take care of details such as arranging a building and pest inspection, selecting a legal conveyancer and dealing with the selling agent on your behalf.

➤ *Building and pest inspection.* If you are buying the property yourself, a building and pest inspection is essential and your initial contract of sale should be made subject to this being to your satisfaction. If the inspection reveals any obvious repairs or replacements that need to be made, you can negotiate a reduction of the sale price — and the vendor is likely to accept because their only alternative is to start the sale process over again with another buyer.

➤ *Conveyancer*. You will need to select a conveyancer to conduct the legal and financial aspects of the sale and process the relevant paperwork on your behalf. There are many who offer a flat fee to do this, so you can shop around.

➤ *Finance*. If you are going to need finance, make your offer subject to receiving finance, and you can also stipulate the kind of finance, such as 'bank finance', so that you are not caught having to accept vendor or other non-bank finance at a higher interest rate. This also gives you an 'escape clause' if something else turns up that changes your mind about proceeding.

➤ *Identification survey*. If you are unsure of how the actual physical location of the property compares to that shown on the title plan, or if it appears that any improvements, such as fences, eaves, garages, or even the dwelling itself may not be situated entirely within the boundaries, or in accordance with local council requirements, you should obtain a land surveyor's identification survey.

➤ *Building and pest inspection*. You should make your offer subject to a satisfactory inspection carried out by a qualified building and pest inspector. Not only will this reveal any structural, drainage and leakage problems as well as evidence of past or present pest infestations, it will enable you to claim a reduction in the offered price to have repairs carried out. The electrical circuitry check may need to be carried out separately.

➤ *Searches*. A title deed search, normally done by the conveyancer, will ensure that the claimed owners do in fact own the property and whether there are any outstanding mortgages or other encumbrances or caveats that could prevent or impede its sale. The search will also show any easements and rights of way on the property relating to public access, drainage, sewerage or transmission lines.

➤ *Body corporate*. If the property is strata titled, you should obtain a statement from the vendor's estate agent showing the amount of body corporate and sinking fund fees that the property is liable for and when they are due, plus the amount of local government rates and utility charges that apply to the property.

➤ *Current lease details*. If the property is currently rented, you need to know the details. The vendor's estate agent should provide you with a statement from the managing agent (if they are different) showing details of who the property is leased to, what the rent payments are, whether they are up to date, when the lease expires and, if this is imminent, whether the tenant wishes to stay.

◆◆◆

When you have determined the right price, made an offer, and that offer is accepted, you have completed the sixth key to successful property investment. This is the point at which many investors take their foot off the pedal, thinking that the hard work has been done. But success is about obtaining the best possible results, which means not just buying the right property at a fair price in the best area, but also selling it at the right time, which is what the seventh and last key shows you.

Key 7

Know the best time to sell

Key 6 showed you how to determine the right price for any property; this last key shows you how to know the best time to sell. This is an essential part of your due diligence, as growth in property values does not continue forever and a few years of high growth in most housing markets is usually followed by many years of little to no growth at all.

You may remember the predictive method we applied in Key 2. Now you simply reverse the strategy to determine the best time to sell, rather than to buy. As described in Key 2, there are five types of markets:

➤ stressed

➤ buyer

➤ neutral

➤ seller

➤ boom.

The sales and listings ratio allows us to read any market, while the trends show us which way the market is moving. Also remember that the five types of housing markets can apply either to house or to unit markets, which should always be considered separately. A suburb may simultaneously have a shortage of houses on the market and a surplus of units listed for sale, and they could be trending in different directions.

How to use sales and listings data

The house and unit market in every suburb can be placed somewhere on the scale shown in table 2.3 on page 40. This position reflects the current supply and demand situation, and it is also usually moving in one direction or the other. This is due in part to the altering relationship of supply and demand for housing in the suburb. We can therefore use exactly the same method of market analysis and prediction as described in detail under the 'Predict short-term price and rent changes' heading on page 36 of Key 2, but reverse the process to help us determine when the best time to sell an investment property has been reached.

This analysis tells us when the local market may be about to enter into conditions where prospective sellers outnumber prospective buyers. It enables us to avoid those unwanted scenarios where time on the market grows slowly while increasingly frustrated prospective sellers wait for the buyers to materialise. It empowers us to sell before vendor discounting becomes more prevalent as the proportion of prospective vendors grows in relation to buyers and bargain hunters move in on stressed sellers. The turning point is when the market is about to change from a seller market to a neutral market — before it reveals those visible signs of deterioration. We do this by regularly reading the market, exactly as explained on page 42 in Key 2 under 'How to generate your own housing market forecasts'. Because we are looking for the telltale signs of when to sell, we only need to do this analysis for those suburbs where our investment properties are located, and for the types of properties we have (i.e. houses or units). Once again we consult the Databank in *Australian Property Investor* magazine to find the annual sales total and then look up the number of current online listings for houses or units for sale in that suburb and compare them according to the ratios shown in table 2.2 on page 39 to determine the type of market.

If you purchased your property in a market where prices are now rising rapidly you need to update your research every month, because boom markets can change quickly, unlike buyer or stressed markets where the numbers of intending sellers far outweighs buyer demand. Naturally, there may be some other considerations that might cause you not to consider selling, such as a high rental yield, or the potential for redevelopment. You may have information that suggests that the suburb may be about to boom for other reasons. Analysing changes in the ratio and trend of sales and listings provides you with a way of measuring the effects of changes in supply and demand, and as such acts as a sort of early warning system. It should never be taken in isolation as providing a cause for expected change.

How to track the supply side

The supply side of the housing market is made up of both listings and new stock. Listings comprise the sum of properties for sale on the market and we can often accurately estimate the current and expected performance of a local housing market by comparing the number of listed properties to the demand for similar properties. In other words, if the demand is greater than the supply, prices may rise, and vice versa. But when significant quantities of new stock and even yet-to-be-built stock come onto the market, the game can change completely and often results in unexpected outcomes for property investors. Too much new stock, called 'overdevelopment' or 'oversupply' (as explained in Key 2), is blamed for price falls and high rental vacancy rates, but these are often caused by falling demand as well.

Supply, and lots of it, is the means by which Australia's cities and towns have grown and been rejuvenated. Older European and American cities have famous cores of heritage suburbs and buildings providing a unique cultural link to the past, but Australia's were founded much more recently on harbours, rivers and bays suited for both security and supply. As its cities grew so did the docks, railways, power stations and abattoirs hugging waterside areas. Much of the potentially most attractive parts of major cities became heavily polluted industrial heartlands and residential no-go zones. But look around these areas today and you'll see a fundamental change reaching almost everywhere as the last decaying and derelict wharf, warehouse and factory precincts are transformed into exciting, vibrant suburbs with new high-rise unit complexes located right on the city's doorstep. This is the supply side of Australia's housing market operating at its best.

Intensive, planned and often overdue medium- to high-density housing developments change the nature of whole suburbs in a positive way. Not only are they attractively situated, the units are also designed with state-of-the-art features and lifestyle facilities specifically appealing to younger renters. Little wonder that, as figure 7.1 shows, rented apartments have become the most popular form of inner urban accommodation in and around major central business districts.

Figure 7.1: rented units dominate inner urban housing markets

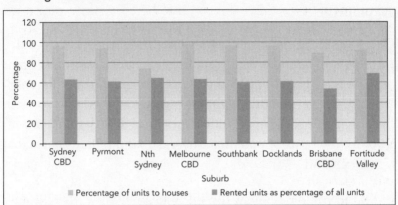

Source: Property Power Database, Property Power Partners.

In fact, units now make up well over 90 per cent of housing stock in the eastern and northern capital city inner-urban centres and comprise over half in the other capital city central business districts. Private investors own over 60 per cent of them, because they make such obvious investment choices. Uniquely located in areas with the highest possible demand for rentals, project marketers vigorously promote such new unit developments to national and international investors to obtain continuous price rises.

Yet something went amiss in many of these locations with investors taking losses in 2013 and 2014 when they sold, with rent demand remaining static at best. Inner Melbourne fared the worst, with unit markets suffering price or rent falls and in some cases both, while performance elsewhere was patchy and sluggish. At the same time, housing markets are being flooded with new high-rise developments in the same areas. Many of these are sold to investors and this means that it is the rental demand that will ultimately determine the success or otherwise of investments made in such areas. As long as there are shortages of rental stock, rents keep rising and this causes the rental yield to rise as well. The high yield then attracts more investors and so prices start increasing as they compete with each other for properties.

Oversupplies of rental properties have the reverse effect, and if price rises in suburbs with forecast rental stock surpluses occur at all, they will be subdued and won't last very long before prices fall. The reason for this is that things are not as they seem in these markets, with supply-side issues caused by developers who work on the basis of potential buyer demand rather than actual renter demand.

Always check real market conditions, actual rental demand and price predictions from a reputable and independent source before committing to anything and remember that incentives and guarantees are not part of a property's real market value. You can do your own research as well, because the supply side tends to operate according to set patterns of recurring events over time, allowing you to estimate where your suburb is positioned.

Supply lags behind demand and creates hidden surpluses

One of the most common traps that investors fall into is being persuaded to buy into new developments, especially off-the-plan high-rise-unit blocks, without understanding the risks they present. The biggest threat posed by such investments is what I call the *hidden surplus*. The process starts when a new area is slated for urban renewal or refurbishment. Because developers need finance, they will pre-sell enough properties as early as possible 'off the plan' to get finance underway. Purchasers may commit with a small deposit bond, and settlement might be years away, with plenty of time to flip or trade the property if prices rise in the interim. If investors retain their properties they may have several more years of protection under a rental guarantee before the true rental situation takes hold. At the same time developments sell out and further projects are started so the stock of new properties keeps growing based on the premise of continued rising rental demand. By the time a stock oversupply becomes apparent, it may have already been in existence for several years, but not evident. Figure 7.2 shows how new unit development in a typical inner urban suburb is based on earlier demand trends and results in huge surpluses, in this case from 2008 to 2011, caused by overdevelopment during the previous years.

Figure 7.2: supply lags behind demand

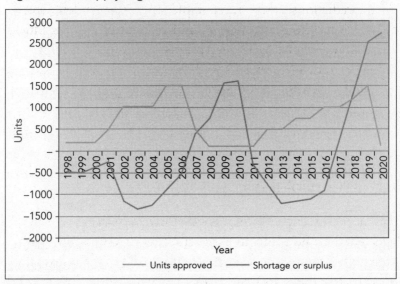

Source: Property Power Database, Property Power Partners.

Even if the housing shortage worsens in most capital city locations, the lag effect can cause the opposite where large new developments are concentrated. Once the oversupply has become apparent because of falling prices and rents, new developments drop away and it can take several years before developers are bold enough to re-enter such a market even after another shortage becomes evident.

There's a right time to sell, so in addition to using the supply and demand methods revealed above to estimate when that might be, it is imperative for you to be aware of possible supply-side changes that will affect the saleability and future price of your property. See page 120 in Key 4, under the heading 'Conduct on-the-ground research', for how to check for signs of overdevelopment. Periodically check with the local council so you'll know when development applications are placed and the timelines for sales and occupation. Regularly consult online listing sites for new or off-the-plan house or unit listings. What often initially appears as one listing on the real estate listing site may conceal a potential development of several hundred units or land subdivision, revealed when you go to the developer's or project marketer's site to see their plans for future development of the project. Finally, check rental trends in areas with high numbers of rented properties, watching for changes in the number of rental vacancies and median asking rents over time. If you notice the number of vacancies increasing over some months, asking rents may start dropping and ultimately lead to a falling away of investor demand in the suburb with consequent price falls.

This early warning system can save you from disasters before prices start to fall from overdevelopment or falling renter demand. You can also effectively use the supply-side analysis methods shown on page 107 under the heading 'Off-the-plan and speculative investment' in Key 4. These methods will point you in the opposite direction to areas where supply limits have been reached and rental demand is rising—conditions perfect for property investment.

How to find the best 'buy and hold' investment areas

What if you don't want to sell? Although the housing market provides its best returns to investors who ride waves of growth by buying in areas where prices are about to rise and then selling when the growth is about to stop, there are some investors who must invest for long periods of time for other reasons, such as to meet beneficiary, trust and superannuation fund requirements. This raises the question: are there some areas of the housing market that consistently perform better than others over long periods of time, such as eight years or more, and if there are, how can you find them? Many proponents of the 'buy and hold' theory would in fact argue that while some suburbs may lead and others will lag, housing market growth eventually evens out everywhere and if growth in your neck of the woods hasn't occurred yet it means that you haven't waited long enough. This theory is totally misleading because it is completely incorrect. The long-term growth of a few types of housing in certain locations has been consistently and significantly higher than in others and there is nothing to suggest that such trends will not continue in future.

First, capital city housing prices grow more than in country locations. Australians prefer to live in large cities and this growing urbanisation generates ever-growing demand for housing in already heavily populated and overdeveloped coastal areas. This adds to infrastructure development and maintenance costs as well as creating more or less continuous housing shortages in most of our capital cities. Figure 7.3 (overleaf) indicates that this was not always the case, and in fact around the time of Federation in 1901 the average price of regional and country housing was equal to and in some areas greater than the cost of equivalent city properties.

Figure 7.3: country house prices as a percentage of city house prices 1901 to 2013

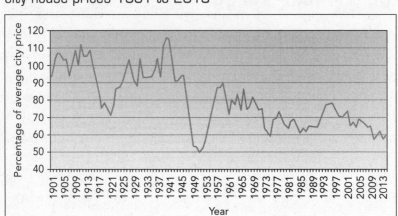

Source: Australian National Library online Trove facility; Mitchell Library archives.

During the First World War from 1917 to 1920 large numbers of men departed country locations to serve their country and this led to a dramatic fall in country house prices when compared to city prices. Following the war, rural housing markets recovered and even briefly boomed, but when the same thing occurred again during the Second World War, this led to an even greater comparative fall in demand, from which country housing markets have never really recovered. A large cause of the rise in city prices from the end of the war onwards was the arrival of large number of overseas migrants, who preferred to live in cities, especially Sydney and Melbourne. Over time, this has resulted in city house prices being higher than those in country towns and figure 7.3 shows how country and regional housing prices have declined to around 60 per cent of capital city equivalents. This is unlikely to change in coming years, with no significant or serious decentralised housing initiatives forthcoming from governments at any level. It does not mean that country prices are falling in real terms, but that their rate of growth is less than that of capital city housing markets. The annual average growth rate of capital city housing markets is about 2 per cent more than country areas on average, which means that investors seeking long-term growth should invest only in larger capital cities unless there is some compelling reason to believe that growth in a regional or rural market will be exceptional.

Second, units have traditionally been viewed as a less desirable purchase option for both owner-occupiers and investors, but as the price of houses in major capital cities pushes them out of the reach of most home buyers, units are becoming more attractive to both investors and owner-occupiers. The introduction of strata title for unit owners in the late 1960s made them more attractive to investors, and figure 7.4 shows that home unit prices have steadily risen since the 1930s from 60 per cent of median house prices to about 90 per cent at present. The current price differential is less than 10 per cent and is reducing as units become a more attractive dwelling option for increasing numbers of households.

Figure 7.4: performance of unit vs house prices 1938 to now

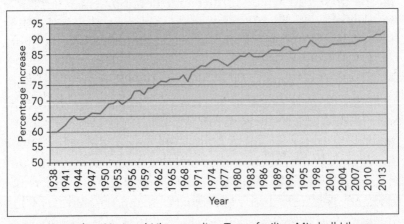

Source: Australian National Library online Trove facility; Mitchell Library archives.

Not only have the quality and fittings of units improved over time, they provide occupiers with the opportunity of living in areas where house prices make them virtually unobtainable, such as beachside, bayside and riverside locations, near shops and transport and many have views that far exceed those of nearby houses. Many modern units are becoming the preferred type of accommodation for both young professionals and retirees, being far less work to maintain than a house. There is also another dynamic at work, which is that nearly half of our population have at least one overseas born parent and their origins in many cases have been countries where units are the normal style of dwelling. This is turning units into a preferred type of accommodation, especially for renters. The results of our research shows that long-term growth is likely to be highest in new unit markets located in high demand areas of capital cities, but are there any other factors that can further narrow down our search?

The ongoing popularity of inner suburban new units is not restricted to buyers and renters. They are also sought after by developers precisely because of this expected demand. This means that areas where further unit development is probable or even possible should be avoided. Although it is impossible to forecast such potential developments over the long term, there are certain precincts in our larger capital cities which obviously have exhausted their potential for further medium or high rise development. We can therefore narrow down the search for consistently better than median performing housing markets to inner suburban capital city new unit markets where further development appears to be exhausted. There is only one more dynamic to be considered, and that is the ongoing rental demand. Not only does high rental demand raise rental yields, it encourages more investment which in turn leads to price rises.

It is important to buy in an area with high rental demand by the right type of renters — young high-income professionals. You can best do this research on the ground by checking with local agents and taking a tour of the area to see what the demographics of typical tenants reveal. You can see that for long-term housing investments, choosing the right type of property in the best area is just as crucial as it is for short term investment success. Remember that differences in long term growth can be substantial and that they are incremental, so that a bad decision gets worse over time, while a good choice gets even better.

How to tell when further growth is unlikely in a market

Australia is a huge market area and its climate varies from northern tropics to dry deserts in the centre and cool temperate regions in the south. This variety enables us to commercially harvest virtually any crops or commodities but also exposes parts of our market to natural disasters such as floods, bushfires, cyclones and droughts. While capital cities are less susceptible to these calamities, they do regularly occur in regional and rural areas and it is essential that you know how housing markets suffer and recover from these events. Natural disasters, from floods to drought and bushfires, are unwelcome but perpetual guests and can cause great devastation and the loss of homes, livelihoods and sometimes even lives. The impact of their possible occurrence is something that all of us, including investors, need to be aware of and take into account when we are considering the purchase or sale of Australian property, and from an investment perspective we need to be aware of the way in which housing markets recover from such disasters.

Bushfires

Perhaps the greatest and most feared danger to homes and their occupants comes from bushfires, because of the destructive fury that has devastated whole communities lying in their paths. While the Australian bush has evolved to cope with fires and even make use of them to germinate and quickly revegetate blackened landscapes, we humans have not yet devised ways of gaining any such advantage.

A horrific example of what bushfires can do is Black Saturday in 2009. Over 2000 homes were lost, 3500 other buildings were destroyed, thousands more were damaged and nearly 200 people lost their lives. Many of the homes destroyed or damaged on Black Saturday were located in some of the most picturesque locations of Victoria, which are still recovering from the effects of the devastation. Following the fires, house prices fell quickly and dramatically in the affected areas. After a slight recovery during the winter of 2009, there were further falls prior to the summer of 2009–10 and little growth up to the summer of 2010–11, but since then the growth rate of the worst-affected towns has exceeded that of the housing markets in other nearby towns. It took several summers without further fire outbreaks to help heal some of the trauma and restore the confidence of homebuyers. Although recovery in such areas can be painful and slow, it inevitably occurs, because when the forests return their natural beauty to these areas they are once again peaceful and picturesque. Towns in traditional fire-risk localities of Victoria have achieved high average annual capital growth rates in the last few years, because as the bush slowly regrows, so does the appeal of these locations.

Droughts

Of all natural disasters, droughts have historically had the greatest economic impact on Australians, because of our dependence on what the land produces. As a result of the Millennium drought, major towns in irrigation areas in the Riverland, Riverina, Sunraysia and Murray/Goulburn Valley localities suffered negative population growth as employment opportunities in picking, packing and processing plants fell and people left to find work elsewhere. The resultant falls in demand caused a slow but steady drop in house prices throughout these localities. From 2009 the waters returned to the rivers and the dams and storages filled again. The local towns received increased tourism, more retirees are arriving and there's renewed economic prosperity. House price-growth returned to some of the towns and then spread to the others, but once house prices caught up to other unaffected areas this bounce-back effect stopped and the rate of growth declined.

Unfortunately, even as the rains brought relief to farmers in the south of the country, the source of the water created a different set of challenges for home owners in the northern coastal regions.

Cyclones

Forming in the monsoonal trough north of Australia between December and April, an average of ten cyclones hit the Australian coast each year. Luckily, most of these are not in major populated areas and their impact is usually limited to crop damage and transport disruptions. Our most severe recent cyclone was Yasi, which hit the north Queensland coast in early 2011 and caused widespread damage to coastal towns. Gradually turning into a tropical rain depression as it moved south-west over Queensland, Yasi dumped torrential rains that resulted in local flooding in South Australia and Victoria. Towns and settlements in Queensland's northern coastal areas that were directly in its path such as Mission Beach, Innisfail, Gordonvale and Tully suffered severe property damage and prices crashed.

Falls in prices occurred within a few months, but unlike the slow recovery of fire or drought affected areas, housing markets recovered within a year. This is due to the localised nature of damage that cyclones cause and the fact that building codes in high-risk areas are stringent and houses are built to withstand all but the most intense cyclonic activity. Investors should only buy properties built to the code, ensure that they have adequate insurance cover and maintain a contingency fund to cover loss of rental income during cyclone threats. The risk to investors is more related to the disruption of mining activities and port shutdowns from cyclone warnings than it is to potential loss of property.

Flooding

The location of most of our coastal and inland cities on rivers means that the risk of flooding is always present, but the severity and extent of flooding throughout eastern Australia in recent years has been unprecedented. The worst summer was 2010–11, when a series of disastrous floods inundated many of Queensland's regional towns and cities, including much of Brisbane. Widespread flooding also occurred in many parts of New South Wales and Victoria. Flash floods can occur virtually anywhere, resulting in total property losses and tragic loss of life due to their unexpected nature.

Housing markets in such areas behave much like those hit by bushfires, but housing markets in areas that are located in demonstrated flood-prone areas and in areas where flooding is less unpredictable behave differently to those hit by fires or cyclones. River levels are monitored and warning systems are in place to protect lives and minimise stock and property losses. Flood damage does not usually result in total building losses, as dwellings are constructed both to withstand flood surges and minimise water damage. When the waters have subsided, the long cleanup process begins and it is not until the locality is back to its former appearance that the housing market surges forward once again, but then it does so rather quickly. In Rockhampton, floods in 1967, 2002, 2008 and 2010 caused a halt to price-growth which in each case lasted up to two years and was then followed by dramatic house price increases. The expected price rise in 2010 did not occur due to the recurrence of flooding within the two-year recovery period, so the anticipated price catch-up may be twice as large and may take twice as long. The implications for areas that are affected by severe flooding is that it takes a long time for recovery in their housing markets to occur and this is usually when buyers least anticipate it. The reason is that it takes time not just to restore houses and localities, but also to replace recollections of the flooding with happier, more recent events. Because many flood-affected suburbs and towns are located in what would normally be highly sought-after areas, the localities that have suffered the greatest falls in house prices after floods are likely to achieve the highest growth when confidence and recovery return.

The point to all this research is that it indicates that once housing prices in areas affected by floods, fires or drought have caught up to other unaffected areas, further growth is unlikely, and because of the length of time that has elapsed since the disaster occurred, most analysts are unaware of the reason for the higher price-growth and are at a loss as to why it has occurred.

It has been my aim in this book to show you that property investment can be successful at any time, under any market conditions, anywhere in Australia. I don't mean by this that every property investment will be successful all the time everywhere, but simply that every suburb or town in Australia has the potential to provide you with excellent property investment results if you use the right strategy at the right time. Even when housing markets falter there are opportunities and it is often when a market has lost all appeal to buyers that it may offer the best opportunities for investors.

It is all about adopting a housing investment strategy that is best suited to the prevailing type of market, whether it be renovating in a neutral market, riding growth waves in a seller market, flipping in boom markets or buying properties at bargain prices in buyer and stressed markets. My hope is that this book enables you to successfully use the tips, techniques and strategies I have researched, tested and refined so that you get the best possible results from your property investments.

Further resources

Resources available to property investors range from free suburb reports to fee-based online research tools. They are easy for you to find by using Google searches with keywords such as 'housing', 'property' and 'investment'. Some of the sites offer reports, webinars, seminars, boot camps and other education services and you need to be wary of those promoting their services for 'free', as they might be thinly disguised fronts for developers and project marketers promoting properties from which they receive a commission, kickback, finder's fee or other incentive. It is essential that you find out who is providing the information and who is paying them to provide it, either by searching their websites or by simply asking them the question. Never rely on any service unless the claims made are supported by documented evidence of their past accuracy and total independence.

Australian Bureau of Statistics

The Australian Bureau of Statistics is a statutory government authority that is charged with collecting and making available statistics on a huge range of economic, financial, business and demographic subjects. All property investors should use their free online site, QuickStats, which provides population, household and housing data for suburbs, towns and cities. But remember that this data comes from the Population and Housing Census, which is only conducted every five years, such as 2011 and 2016. It takes a year for the data to be updated in QuickStats. Because many housing market reports refer to population, housing and income stats derived from the last census, the data could be up to six years old. Established suburbs and older regional areas may not change much over this time, but the housing markets of new suburban areas and inner urban unit developments can dramatically alter in a few years. You can access QuickStats at www.abs.gov.au (QuickStats is located in the Census Home menu).

Housing data providers

Residential property data providers collect housing data such as past and present housing values, sale prices, rents, time on market and number of sales for properties, suburbs and cities. They provide free and other paid reports and services on the housing market for investors, including property, street and suburb reports and services. Two commonly used providers are:

➤ Australian Property Monitors: www.homepriceguide.com.au

➤ CoreLogic RP Data: www.myrp.com.au

Property listings information providers

Virtually all properties listed for sale or rent feature on one or more online listings sites. They give you information on asking prices and rents, the number and type of properties for sale in an area, and also have some analytical data, such as recent sales data. The two most commonly used are:

➤ www.realestate.com.au

➤ www.domain.com.au.

Property investment magazines

Australian Property Investor

Australian Property Investor (API) is an independent monthly property investment publication and is Australia's most widely read monthly magazine for property investors, homebuyers, small developers and property professionals. Each issue contains features, case studies of successful investors and small developers, investment and renovation tips and strategies, as well as regional and suburb profiles. The Databank section at the back of each copy provides a complete set of data showing current and historical house and unit prices, sales, asking rents and vacancy rates for every suburb with sufficient properties to enable accurate data to be presented. The housing price and sales data contained in the Databank is provided by Australian Property Monitors.

For more information visit www.apimagazine.com.au.

Your Investment Property

This is another popular resource for property investors, also published monthly and sold at newsagents and by annual subscription. It has similar content to *API* magazine, and the Property Price Guide at the back of each copy provides a complete set of data showing current and historical house and unit prices, sales, asking rents and vacancy rates for every suburb with sufficient properties to enable accurate data to be presented. The data is provided by CoreLogic RP Data and because each data provider has their own method of calculating sales and median prices, some of the data may be different from that provided by *API* magazine. The rule is to be consistent, and only use one data source.

For more information visit www.yourinvestmentpropertymag. com.au.

E-newsletters

There are hundreds of e-newsletters and blogs available to investors that will provide some general information about the housing market. All of the major data providers, buyer's agents, mortgage brokers, mentors and motivators have their own newsletter and there are others provided by self-interest groups such as developers, project marketers and seller's agents as well as those supported by advertising.

Be wary of free newsletters that are promotional fronts for spruikers and talking heads or those with hidden agendas. The common feature in such newsletters is an emphasis on the person, not their credentials, promises of wealth from property investment without any real explanation or examples of how this can be obtained. They will invariably offer a free report, webinar or workshop where all will be revealed. You can subscribe to some of the most useful e-newsletters on these sites:

➤ Housing Heads UP: www.understandproperty.com.au

➤ Australian Property Investor Newsletter: www.apimagazine.com.au

➤ Housing Industry Association Media Releases: www.hia.com.au

➤ Michael Yardney's Property Update: www.propertyupdate.com.au

➤ My RPData Property Pulse: www.corelogic.com.au

➤ RBA News: www.rba.gov.au

➤ Property Observer: www.propertyobserver.com.au.

Mentoring services

Mentoring organisations aim to provide investors with ongoing support and hands-on assistance and keep them motivated to succeed. This is particularly useful for investors who plan to add value to their properties through renovations or developments, as there are many traps for the unwary in these fields. The only mentoring company that I can recommend through personal association is Results Mentoring. They provide one-on-one mentoring by highly experienced property investors covering all aspects of property investment. You can see what mentoring companies such as Results Mentoring offer at www.ResultsMentoring.com/UnlockingThePropertyMarket.

Educators

Property education services such as online webinars and tutorials or face-to-face boot camps and short courses are offered free of charge and for a fee. Free education services may actually be fronts for buyer or seller agents, so always check the motives of the providers as well as their experience, expertise and qualifications. The only property education with which I am associated is the 7steps2success course, an online property investment education program presented through a series of videos, slide presentations, written lessons, templates, games and quizzes. The content is designed to provide students with an understanding of how the housing market works and deliver practical applications so that investors can obtain the best results from property investment. For more information, visit www.7steps2success.com.au.

Glossary

This glossary explains the meanings of terms in this book or that you may come across while researching the housing market.

actual rent   the gross rent being paid for a property to the owner

apartment (also *unit* or *flat*)   one of several dwellings in a block usually owned under strata (or company) title

asking rent   the current advertised rent for a property

capital gain   the capital growth realised when an asset is sold

capital growth   the increase in the value of an asset over time

days on market   (see *time on market*)

demographics   the size of a population, its composition, development, distribution and change

dwelling a building primarily used by households for residential accommodation, which can include a house, unit, apartment, duplex, townhouse or villa unit

fair market value the price that a property is likely to sell for, based on recent comparable sales evidence

flat (also *unit* or *apartment*) one of several dwellings in a block usually owned under strata (or company) title

households a number of people living together, such as couples, two-parent and single-parent families, groups (such as mining workers or students) or sole occupants, known as singles

housing general term for places where households live, including units, flats, apartments, houses, caravan parks, hospices and jails

housing commission housing that state government authorities set up in the postwar period to provide affordable housing for low-income families, also known as public housing

leasing renting a property under a written agreement

listing the public advertising of a property for sale

market value the highest price that a property is likely to sell for, usually established by agreement between the vendor and the listing agent, who will describe this as the 'fair market value'

mean (also *average*) the middle value of a set of numbers

median the middle number in a set of numbers

median sale price the middle number in sales over a set time period for a certain area

median value the middle number in values at a set time for a certain area

negative gearing when income from a property (usually rent) is not sufficient to cover costs associated with ownership, such as loan repayments, maintenance, rates and management fees; the benefit is that the interest on loan repayments for investment properties is an allowable tax deduction

off the plan purchase of a property before it has been completed, or in some cases even commenced

old system title a precursor to torrens title that is still come across in older suburbs; it consists of a description of the property and its origins, from the original grant or purchase through to the present

on the market properties that are listed for sale

property land that can be leased or sold under a separate title

positive gearing when the income from a property (usually rent) is more than sufficient to cover costs associated with ownership, such as loan repayments, maintenance, rates and management fees, resulting in a net return to the owner

private treaty a property sale conducted by the vendor and buyer privately

rent (see also *asking rent* and *actual rent*) the cost of leasing a property paid by the tenant to the owner

rent rate (see *rental yield*)

rent return (see *rental yield*)

rental yield (also *rent rate* and *rent return*) the current gross annual return to the owner from rental income on an investment expressed as a percentage of the purchase price of the investment

residential the zoning of land for residential purposes

residential property dwellings that are located on residentially zoned land

return   the profit made from an investment

strata title   the title system used for units, flats, apartments and some townhouses and villas that limits title to each individual unit, and places ownership, administration and maintenance of the block's exterior and common property areas under the control of the body corporate

tenancy   the period of time a property is leased

tenant   the person leasing or renting a property

time on market   the period of time taken from its first listing for a property to sell

torrens title   the most common system of freehold title used in Australia, which provides a plan showing the location and dimensions of the property

total return   the combination capital growth and rent return obtained over a given period of time

townhouse   a dwelling that is either considered to be a unit or house depending on the title system used, i.e. either strata for units or torrens for houses

unit (also *flat* or *apartment*)   one of several dwellings in a block usually owned under strata (or company) title

valuation   a written estimate of a property's worth, usually supplied to the lender by a sworn valuer, used to determine the actual loan-to-value ratio and whether loan mortgage insurance is required

vendor   a property owner who places their property on the market

vendor discounting   the difference between the initial listed asking price for a property and the amount for which it is actually sold

Index

Adelaide 10, 133
affordability 12, 34, 66, 70
Australian Bureau of Statistics 174
Australian Property Investor 40, 42,
    175, 177
Australian Property Investor Databank
    38, 78, 157, 175

baby boomers 8
bargains 51, 95, 105–108
Basic Community Profile 78
boom and bust 9, 29, 52, 53, 113,
    143
boom markets 4, 10–11, 13, 16, 36,
    37, 38–41, 45–47, 51–53, 55–58,
    61, 62, 66, 67–69, 70–71, 72,
    73–74, 76, 77, 78, 95, 99–101,
    102–103, 104–105, 107, 108–118,
    141–143, 156, 157, 164, 172
Brisbane 10, 82, 142, 159, 170

bubbles, housing price 58, 59,
    85–86, 144
building and pest inspection 152,
    153
bushfires, effect of 168, 171
buy, time to 2, 15, 41, 59, 63–93
buy and hold strategy 2, 6, 9, 104
    — best areas for 163–167
buyer and seller markets
    — first-home buyers 22, 23, 26, 28,
        64–69, 93, 99, 100–101, 107
    — investors 13–18, 21, 22, 23, 24,
        26, 29, 31, 32, 36, 47, 69, 70,
        79–93
    — retirees 22, 23, 26, 28, 32, 61,
        64, 73–78, 97, 98, 99, 107,
        113, 118, 132, 166, 169
    — upgraders 22–24, 28, 68,
        69–73, 99
buyer's agent 152, 176

capital cities 8, 15, 58, 77, 92, 166,
    167; *see also* suburbs; entries
    under city names
— data 30–31, 32
— drift to 21, 26–28, 82
— housing shortages 21, 29,
    161–162
— housing stock 132, 159, 166
— prices 5–7, 9–11, 23, 78,
    163–165
— tourism 115–116
capital growth 14, 26, 28, 50, 91,
    109, 125, 168
China
— mining 55
— tourism 110, 114–116
choice of property
— active growth from renovation
    125, 130–135
— aims 125–138
— bargains 95, 105–108
— facilities in area 120–121, 122
— high cash flow 125, 136–138
— household preferences 95, 96,
    97
— imminent price growth 98–101,
    103
— narrowing the search 95–123
— next boom market 108–118
— passive growth 125, 128–130
— price to pay 139–154
— rental growth 136–138
— research 118–123
— splash effect 95, 101–103
— what to buy 125–138
— when to buy 63–93
— where to buy 63–93, 95–123
— wrong 97
cohort effect 68

construction company
    accommodation strategies 60–61
consumer confidence 12, 34
conveyancing 153
cyclones, effect of 169–170

data 35, 36–41, 44, 45, 48–49, 145,
    146–147, 174; *see also* ratios
— census 32, 34, 88, 90, 174
— listings 39–40
— median price 42–43, 78, 148
— providers 41, 148, 174–177
— rental market 88–91
— sales 42–43
— sales/listings ratios 43, 103,
    157
— trends 43–48
— use of 41, 42, 150, 152,
    156–157
data, using
— sales and listings 156–157
— supply lags demand 160–161
— supply side, tracking 157–162
— buy and hold, best areas for
    163–167
demand and supply *see* supply and
    demand
demand dynamics, market 1–2, 19–
    32, 34, 144; *see also* households
    and markets
— people 1, 19, 20–28, 34, 63
— price and rent movements 2,
    34
— properties 1, 19, 30–32, 34, 63
— purchasing power 1, 19, 28–30,
    34, 63
deposit, house purchase 66–67, 68,
    69, 70, 82, 99, 100–101, 104–105,
    160

depressions 4, 21, 29
developers and developments,
    property 4, 48, 49, 51, 54, 59, 62,
    79, 85, 104–105, 106, 107, 113,
    119, 121–122, 147, 157, 158–159,
    160–161, 162, 166, 174, 175,
    176, 177; *see also* infrastructure;
    mining; port development;
    tourism
  — overdevelopment 40–50,
      82–84, 85–86, 109, 116, 121,
      158, 162
  — pre-sales 48, 49, 50, 105,
      107–108, 113, 160–162
differentials, high price 126–127,
    165
discretionary purchases 106, 107
droughts, effect of 12, 168–169,
    171

economy 3, 4–5, 12, 34, 58, 66, 71,
    75, 82, 107, 110, 111, 114, 142,
    168, 169, 174
employment 12, 23, 26, 27, 34, 71,
    75, 83, 111–112, 121, 122, 136,
    139
e-newsletters 176–177

fair market value 39, 139, 148–149,
    150, 152
finance and loans, housing 5, 11,
    12, 16, 20, 28, 29, 30, 32, 34, 64,
    66–68, 69–70, 71, 74–75, 82, 93,
    99, 101, 105, 106, 107, 108, 153,
    160
first-home buyers 22, 23, 26,
    28, 64–69, 93, 99, 100–101,
    107
Five Dock (NSW) 102, 103

flip and trade 95, 104–105
floods, effect of 170–171
forecasts 12–13, 18, 31, 33–34, 63,
    82, 90, 101, 160, 166; *see also*
    prediction
  — accurate 40, 47–48,
  — generating your own 42–50,
      157
  — ratio sales to total properties
      38–39, 43–48

gearing, positive 16–17
gentrification 96, 133
Gladstone (Qld) boom and bust 4,
    52–53, 80, 84, 146
government incentives 66, 69,
    100–101, 160
Global Financial Crisis 12, 57, 75,
    113, 114
Gold Coast housing 4, 49, 73, 108,
    113, 115, 116
growth potential 1, 17, 18, 26,
    33–62, 95, 100, 108, 109, 116,
    128–135
growth unlikely 167–171

Hay (NSW)
  — lessons from changing
      historical data 4–12
  — rental properties and prices
      86–88, 90–91
  — sales and listings tracked
      46–47
homes, former holiday 17, 25, 29,
    81, 96, 130–132
Hobart 10, 26–28, 56, 132
housing commission properties,
    former 17, 25, 29, 81, 96, 130,
    132–133

household preferences 95, 96, 97
— first-home buyers 99–101, 106, 107
— growth dynamics 98–101
— professional couples 97
— retirees 97, 99
— students 97
— upgraders 99
— young families 97
households and markets 11; *see also* buyer and seller markets
— demand dynamics 1, 19–32
— first-home buyers 22, 23, 26, 28, 64–69, 93, 99, 100–101, 107
— new 65
— operation of 1–12
— overseas arrivals 17, 25, 29, 65, 82, 83, 136
— owner-occupiers 23–24, 32, 48, 58, 63, 70–71, 80, 81, 84, 109, 165
— renters 11–12, 16–18, 22, 24, 25, 28, 60, 79–93, 144
— retirees 22, 23, 26, 28, 32, 61, 64, 73–78, 97, 98, 99, 107, 113, 118, 132, 169
— types of 21–28
— upgraders 22–24, 28, 68, 69–73, 99

identification survey 153
inflation and housing prices 3, 5, 7–9, 148
infrastructure development 12, 16, 50–59, 83, 88, 106, 108, 119, 122, 163
— construction phase 53, 60–61
— speculation phase 53–59

interest rates 12, 66, 67, 68, 69, 70–71, 75, 93, 106, 107
investors 11, 75; *see also* households, renters; rental markets
— markets 13–18, 21, 22, 23, 24, 26, 29, 31, 32, 36, 47, 69, 70, 79–93
— overdevelopment and 48–50
— price to pay 139–154
— rental markets 79–93
— research 118–123
— speculation 1, 13, 50–62, 107–108
— strategies 2, 13, 14, 17, 28, 47, 79, 100, 101, 104–106, 108–118
— time to sell 154, 155–172
— types of 13–18
— what to buy 125–138

Katoomba boom and bust 142–143

lag effect 92–93, 161
lagging indicators 41, 47
Launceston 26–28, 56
Leichhardt (NSW) 102, 103
listings, sources of information 175
loan repayments 66–67, 70, 108
loans and lending *see* finance
location 3, 14, 17, 21, 22, 23, 24, 25, 51, 55, 59, 60, 61, 64, 68, 69, 70–71, 74–78 , 79, 80, 83, 84, 89, 91, 97, 98, 99, 106, 109, 110–118, 119, 126, 130, 131, 132, 135, 137, 140, 141, 145, 149, 150, 153, 159, 161, 163–164, 166, 168, 170

magazines, property investment 175–176
market conditions 45–47

market dynamics 64–78

markets *see also* households and markets; renters

—boom 4, 10–11, 13, 16, 36, 37, 38–41, 45–47, 50–53, 55–58, 61, 62, 66, 67–69, 70–71, 72, 73–74, 76, 77, 78, 95, 99–101, 102–103, 104–105, 107, 108–118, 141–143, 156, 157, 164, 172

—buyer 11–12, 16, 22, 24, 36, 37, 39, 40, 46, 70, 72, 93, 95, 105–108, 148, 155, 157, 172

—changing 45–47

—first-home buyer 64–69

—five types 36–41, 155–156

—investors 109

—neutral 36, 37, 39, 40, 41, 42, 46, 72, 103, 105, 155, 157, 172

—owner-occupiers 109

—ratio of sales to listings 103

—ratio of sales to total properties 38–39, 43–48

—retiree 73–78

—seller 11–12, 16, 22, 24, 32, 36, 37, 38, 39, 40, 41, 46, 47, 70, 72, 103, 130, 148, 152, 156, 157, 172

—stressed 16, 36–37, 39, 40, 45–46, 72, 95, 105–108, 155, 156–157, 172

—upgrader 69–73

median sale prices 15, 18, 35, 41, 46, 47, 91

—misleading 144–147, 148

Melbourne 5, 9, 10, 28, 54, 82, 115, 116, 129, 132, 134, 142, 159, 164

mentoring services 177

migration from overseas 8–9, 12, 17, 25, 29, 64, 65, 66, 82–83, 136, 164–165

Millennium drought 12, 169

mining 170; *see also* infrastructure; speculation

—announcements 16, 57

—towns 18, 25, 26, 29, 49, 55–56, 57–58, 64, 79, 83–84, 90, 106, 122

narrowing your search 95–123

National Infrastructure Construction Schedule 61

natural disasters, effect of 167–171

Newcastle (NSW) 58, 133

offer, making an 152–154

off-the-plan sales 48, 49, 50, 107–108, 113, 162

overdevelopment *see also* infrastructure development

—checking for and recognising 33, 48–50, 121, 162

—risks 48–50, 59, 82, 85, 116, 158, 161, 162

oversupply 48, 49, 105, 108, 113, 121–122, 158, 160, 161–162; *see also* overdevelopment; supply and demand

Perth housing 10

population 12, 58, 60, 76, 78, 116, 117, 166, 169, 174; *see also* migration from overseas

—changes 5, 18, 20–21, 26, 28, 65–66, 74, 81, 88, 142, 169

port development 16, 18, 51–53, 55–56, 57, 58, 83, 84, 85, 89, 90, 108, 142, 170

Port Hedland (WA) boom and bust 52–53, 54–56, 57

prediction 8, 160
— data for 34–35
— difficulty of 3–4, 7, 12–13, 33–35, 49
— methods of 9, 19–32, 36–48, 71–72, 155–156
— short-term price and rent changes 35–41
— systems 19, 20–28, 30–32, 33–34
price(s), property 15, 16, 28–30, *see also* bargains; boom and bust; boom markets; bubbles; median sales price; overdevelopment; rent(al); renters and rental markets; speculation; supply and demand; value
— appropriate 139–154
— capital cities 5–7, 9–11, 23, 78, 163–165
— changes 2, 16, 19–20, 31–32, 63, 86–88, 147, 158–162
— country and regional 54, 163–164
— determining 129–154
— double every eight years myth 2–4, 6–7
— falls 4, 27, 31, 32, 36, 37, 39, 48, 53, 57, 63, 66, 71, 76, 80, 81, 84–85, 87–88, 89, 105–106, 118, 142–144, 145–146, 168–171
— growth 1, 2, 4, 15, 18, 54–58, 64, 73, 75–77, 78, 83–84, 86, 91–93, 98–103, 104–105, 163 109, 108, 113, 135–136, 171
— high differential 126–127, 165
— historical performance 5, 6–12
— inflation and 3, 5, 7–9
— lag effect 92–93, 161
— neutral 36, 37, 41
— overseas migrants 164–165

— predicting 8, 12–13, 33–34, 36–41, 42–48, 63
— purchasing power and 28–30
— renovation, effect of 128–135
— ripple effect 91–93
— rises 2, 4, 7, 10–11, 29, 30, 31, 32, 36, 37, 38–41, 48, 53–57, 60, 68–69, 71–73, 75–76, 79, 85, 87–88, 91, 104–105, 121–122, 139, 142–143, 146–147, 157, 163, 166
— splash effect 95, 101–103
— stability 16–18, 23
— supply and demand, influence of 9–13, 41
— units vs houses 165–166
property managers, questions for 137
purchasing power, rentals vs purchases 28–30

Queanbeyan (NSW), ripple effect in 92–93

railways, influence of 16, 50, 51, 53, 85, 119, 142–143, 158
ratios
— sales/listings ratios (supply/ demand) 38–40, 42, 43, 46, 47, 103, 156, 157
— listings to stock 32, 35
— online search interest 31, 32, 35
— rental vacancies/investor- owned properties 90
real estate agents 97, 120, 148–148
— questions for 135–136
renovation 13, 79, 96, 125, 126–135, 138, 172, 175, 177
— cosmetic improvements 97–98, 126

— ex-holiday homes 130–132
— ex-housing commission 132–133
— old inner suburban houses 134–135
— property choice 126–135
— rent or sell 127
rent(al) *see also* vacancy rates
— changes 19, 20, 29–30, 31–32, 36, 47, 53, 56, 58, 62, 63, 80, 84–93, 118, 143, 156, 158, 159–160
— demand 11, 12, 17, 18, 26, 31, 48, 49, 55, 59, 60–61, 64, 79, 80–84, 85, 87, 88–93, 96, 109, 112, 113, 136–137, 143, 144, 159–162, 166–167
— growth 49, 85–86, 109, 113, 116, 136–138
— guarantee 4, 48, 79, 106, 108, 160, 161
— measuring supply and demand 88–91
— purchasing power and 1, 19, 20, 28–30, 34, 63
— renovation 97–98, 126, 127
— ripple effect 91–93
— shortage/surplus 56, 61, 79, 80, 84–86, 108, 116, 158
— supply and demand 88–93, 160
— units 158–162, 166–7
— vs price levels 11–12
— yields 16–18, 26, 27, 31, 32, 35, 60, 79, 80–83, 85, 86, 87, 91, 157, 166
renters and rental markets 24–30, 32, 59, 63, 122, 158
— casual workers 29, 109, 112
— effect on housing markets 79–80
— four markets 24, 25, 26
— influence on property values 80–893
— moving 84–93
— new households 17, 25, 28, 29, 30, 39, 65, 82, 144
— overseas migrants 17, 25, 29, 65, 82–83, 136, 164–165
— opportunity seekers 25, 29, 64, 83–84, 109–110, 112
— permanent 17, 25, 26, 29, 81–82, 96
— students 83, 97, 109, 178
— suburb types 13–19
— temporary 26, 28–29
— troublesome 136
— types 14, 24, 25, 26, 81–93, 109, 136, 137, 167
research, conducting 36–42, 78, 95
— resources 5, 173–178
ripple effect 91–93, 101, 102
Rockhampton (Qld) 171

searches, property 153–154
sell, time to 2, 47, 59, 62, 70, 104–105, 130, 155–172
shortages, property 10, 18, 19, 21, 38, 39, 44, 55, 56, 58, 89, 61, 72–73, 80–81, 84–85, 89, 90, 99, 103, 116, 143, 144, 156, 161–162, 163
— vs surpluses 30–32
splash effect 95, 101–103
strata title search 154
suburbs
— cash cows 1, 14, 16–18, 19, 24, 26, 79, 82, 83
— features, desirable 96
— features, undesirable 96, 127
— five housing markets 36–41

suburbs *(continued)*
— long shots 1, 14, 15–16, 18, 19, 24, 40
— shooting stars 1, 14, 18, 19, 24, 40, 41
— sleepers 14, 15, 18, 24, 40
— types 14–17
— types of renters 14
— variation across city 71–72
Summer Hill (NSW) 102–103
supply
— side tracking 157–162
— lags demand 160–162
supply and demand 9–12, 13, 21, 30–32, 36, 41, 48, 80, 121, 128, 156, 157, 162
— measure rental 88–91
surplus properties 19, 30–32, 36–37, 38, 39, 44, 60, 72, 73, 80, 84–85, 89, 103, 108, 144, 156, 160–162; *see also* overdevelopment
speculation 2, 15–16, 33, 50–62, 88, 106, 107–108, 109, 141, 143–144, 162; *see also* developers and development; infrastructure
Sydney 5, 9, 10, 28, 67, 70–73, 82, 102, 115–116, 132, 134, 142, 147, 159, 164

Tasmania 26–28; *see also* Hobart; Launceson; Zeehan
tipping point 16, 44, 46
tourism and housing 25, 26, 29, 56, 58, 61, 64, 79, 83, 90, 91, 109–118, 119, 122, 169
Townsville (Qld) 58
trends 40, 42, 43–48

units, home 22, 25, 29, 38, 40, 42, 46, 50, 64, 82, 104, 105, 107,

109, 113, 118, 121, 144, 146–147, 148, 156, 157, 158–162, 165–166

vacancy rates 4, 18, 27, 31, 32, 35, 62, 79, 81, 84–91, 108, 117, 126, 137, 158, 162, 175, 176,
value of property 140–144; *see also* median sale price; price
— analysts' estimation 148–149
— fair market 152
— median sale price 144–147
— your estimation 149–152
Victorian Regional Rail Link 54

what to pay 139–154
— analysts calculation of value 148–149
— current lease details 154
— details to check 152–154
— finance, organising 153
— median sale price 144–147
— offer, making an 152–154
— strata title search 154
— value of land 140–144
— your own estimate 149–152
where to buy 63–93
when to buy 2, 15, 41, 59, 63–9
when to sell 2, 47, 59, 62, 70, 104–105, 130, 155–172

yield
— rental 16–18, 26, 27, 31, 32, 35, 60, 79, 80–83, 85, 86, 87, 91, 157, 166
— source of high 17–18

Zeehan (Tasmania) boom and bust 27, 56–58

Connect
with WILEY ▶▶▶

WILEY

Browse and purchase the full range of Wiley publications on our official website.

www.wiley.com

Check out the Wiley blog for news, articles and information from Wiley and our authors.

www.wileybizaus.com

Join the conversation on Twitter and keep up to date on the latest news and events in business.

@WileyBizAus

Sign up for Wiley newsletters to learn about our latest publications, upcoming events and conferences, and discounts available to our customers.

www.wiley.com/email

Wiley titles are also produced in e-book formats. Available from all good retailers.

WILEY

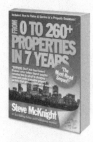